T0301943

An Analysis of

Burton G. Malkiel's

A Random Walk
Down Wall Street

Nick Burton

Published by Macat International Ltd
24:13 Coda Centre, 189 Munster Road, London SW6 6AW.

Distributed exclusively by Routledge
2 Park Square, Milton Park, Abingdon, Oxon OX14 4RN
711 Third Avenue, New York, NY 10017, USA

Routledge is an imprint of the Taylor & Francis Group, an informa business

Copyright © 2017 by Macat International Ltd
Macat International has asserted its right under the Copyright, Designs and Patents Act
1988 to be identified as the copyright holder of this work.

The print publication is protected by copyright. Prior to any prohibited reproduction, storage in
a retrieval system, distribution or transmission in any form or by any means, electronic, mechanical, recording or otherwise, permission should be obtained from the publisher or where
applicable a license permitting restricted copying in the United Kingdom should be obtained
from the Copyright Licensing Agency Ltd, Barnard's Inn, 86 Fetter Lane, London EC4A 1EN, UK.

The ePublication is protected by copyright and must not be copied, reproduced, transferred,
distributed, leased, licensed or publicly performed or used in any way except as specifically
permitted in writing by the publishers, as allowed under the terms and conditions under which
it was purchased, or as strictly permitted by applicable copyright law. Any unauthorised distribution or use of this text may be a direct infringement of the authors and the publishers' rights
and those responsible may be liable in law accordingly.

www.macat.com
info@macat.com

Cataloguing in Publication Data
A catalogue record for this book is available from the British Library.
Library of Congress Cataloguing-in-Publication Data is available upon request.
Cover illustration: A. Richard Allen

ISBN 978-1-912302-28-4 (hardback)
ISBN 978-1-912128-82-2 (paperback)
ISBN 978-1-912281-16-9 (e-book)

Notice
The information in this book is designed to orientate readers of the work under analysis,
to elucidate and contextualise its key ideas and themes, and to aid in the development
of critical thinking skills. It is not meant to be used, nor should it be used, as a
substitute for original thinking or in place of original writing or research. References and
notes are provided for informational purposes and their presence does not constitute
endorsement of the information or opinions therein. This book is presented solely for
educational purposes. It is sold on the understanding that the publisher is not engaged
to provide any scholarly advice. The publisher has made every effort to ensure that
this book is accurate and up-to-date, but makes no warranties or representations with
regard to the completeness or reliability of the information it contains. The information
and the opinions provided herein are not guaranteed or warranted to produce particular
results and may not be suitable for students of every ability. The publisher shall not be
liable for any loss, damage or disruption arising from any errors or omissions, or from
the use of this book, including, but not limited to, special, incidental, consequential or
other damages caused, or alleged to have been caused, directly or indirectly, by the
information contained within.

CONTENTS

THE MACAT LIBRARY

The Macat Library is a series of unique academic explorations of seminal works in the humanities and social sciences – books and papers that have had a significant and widely recognised impact on their disciplines. It has been created to serve as much more than just a summary of what lies between the covers of a great book. It illuminates and explores the influences on, ideas of, and impact of that book. Our goal is to offer a learning resource that encourages critical thinking and fosters a better, deeper understanding of important ideas.

Each publication is divided into three Sections: Influences, Ideas, and Impact. Each Section has four Modules. These explore every important facet of the work, and the responses to it.

This Section-Module structure makes a Macat Library book easy to use, but it has another important feature. Because each Macat book is written to the same format, it is possible (and encouraged!) to cross-reference multiple Macat books along the same lines of inquiry or research. This allows the reader to open up interesting interdisciplinary pathways.

To further aid your reading, lists of glossary terms and people mentioned are included at the end of this book (these are indicated by an asterisk [*] throughout) – as well as a list of works cited.

Macat has worked with the University of Cambridge to identify the elements of critical thinking and understand the ways in which six different skills combine to enable effective thinking.
Three allow us to fully understand a problem; three more give us the tools to solve it. Together, these six skills make up the **PACIER** model of critical thinking. They are:

ANALYSIS – understanding how an argument is built
EVALUATION – exploring the strengths and weaknesses of an argument
INTERPRETATION – understanding issues of meaning

CREATIVE THINKING – coming up with new ideas and fresh connections
PROBLEM-SOLVING – producing strong solutions
REASONING – creating strong arguments

To find out more, visit **WWW.MACAT.COM.**

CRITICAL THINKING AND *A RANDOM WALK DOWN WALL STREET*

Primary critical thinking skill: EVALUATION
Secondary critical thinking skill: ANAYLSIS

Burton Malkiel's 1973 *A Random Walk Down Wall Street* was an explosive contribution to debates about how to reap a good return on investing in stocks and shares. Reissued and updated many times since, Malkiel's text remains an indispensable contribution to the world of investment strategy – one that continues to cause controversy among investment professionals today.

At the book's heart lies a simple question of evaluation: just how successful are investment experts? The financial world was, and is, full of people who claim to have the knowledge and expertise to outperform the markets, and produce larger gains for investors as a result of their knowledge. But how successful, Malkiel asked, are they really? Via careful evaluations of performance – looking at those who invested via 'technical analysis' and 'fundamental analysis' – he was able to challenge the adequacy of many of the claims made for analysts' success. Malkiel found the major active investment strategies to be significantly flawed. Where actively managed funds posted big gains one year, they seemingly inevitably posted below average gains in succeeding years. By evaluating the figures over the medium and long term, indeed, Malkiel discovered that actively-managed funds did far worse on average than those that passively followed the general market index.

Though many investment professionals still argue against Malkiel's influential findings, his exploration of the strengths and weaknesses of the argument for believing investors' claims provides strong evidence that his own passive strategy wins out overall.

ABOUT THE AUTHOR OF THE ORIGINAL WORK

Born in 1932, **Burton G. Malkiel** is one of the most influential American economists specializing in how the stock markets work. After earning an MBA at Harvard University, Malkiel worked for a Wall Street investment firm for a couple of years before moving to academia and gaining a PhD in economics from Princeton. He quickly became a professor, and after a long career is now retired. Malkiel has also acted as a director of many companies, giving him a perspective on both the academic and business worlds. He has served as a member of the Council of Economic Advisers, advising the US president. Malkiel has published numerous books and articles, but is best known for 1973's *A Random Walk Down Wall Street*.

ABOUT THE AUTHOR OF THE ANALYSIS

Dr Nick Burton holds a degree in economics from Bowdoin College, Maine, and a DPhil in English literature from Oxford. An award-winning playwright who has taken on subjects as diverse as the financial crisis and the lives of the Romantic poets, he currently lectures on play-writing at Royal Holloway, University of London, and is the Creative Arts Fellow at Wolfson College, Oxford.

ABOUT MACAT

GREAT WORKS FOR CRITICAL THINKING

Macat is focused on making the ideas of the world's great thinkers accessible and comprehensible to everybody, everywhere, in ways that promote the development of enhanced critical thinking skills.

It works with leading academics from the world's top universities to produce new analyses that focus on the ideas and the impact of the most influential works ever written across a wide variety of academic disciplines. Each of the works that sit at the heart of its growing library is an enduring example of great thinking. But by setting them in context – and looking at the influences that shaped their authors, as well as the responses they provoked – Macat encourages readers to look at these classics and game-changers with fresh eyes. Readers learn to think, engage and challenge their ideas, rather than simply accepting them.

"Macat offers an amazing first-of-its-kind tool for interdisciplinary learning and research. Its focus on works that transformed their disciplines and its rigorous approach, drawing on the world's leading experts and educational institutions, opens up a world-class education to anyone."

Andreas Schleicher
Director for Education and Skills, Organisation for Economic Co-operation and Development

'Macat is taking on some of the major challenges in university education … They have drawn together a strong team of active academics who are producing teaching materials that are novel in the breadth of their approach.'

Prof Lord Broers,
former Vice-Chancellor of the University of Cambridge

'The Macat vision is exceptionally exciting. It focuses upon new modes of learning which analyse and explain seminal texts which have profoundly influenced world thinking and so social and economic development. It promotes the kind of critical thinking which is essential for any society and economy. This is the learning of the future.'

Rt Hon Charles Clarke, former UK Secretary of State for Education

'The Macat analyses provide immediate access to the critical conversation surrounding the books that have shaped their respective discipline, which will make them an invaluable resource to all of those, students and teachers, working in the field.'

Professor William Tronzo, University of California at San Diego

WAYS IN TO THE TEXT

KEY POINTS

- Burton G. Malkiel is an American academic and investor who started as an analyst on Wall Street before moving to a very successful academic career.

- *A Random Walk Down Wall Street* argues that movements in stock* market prices are completely unpredictable, or "random."*

- The book is an argument for the efficient market hypothesis* (EMH), according to which no investor can consistently "beat the market," since in today's world, all legally obtained information that can affect stock prices is almost instantly available to all investors.

Who Is Burton G. Malkiel?

Burton G. Malkiel, the author of *A Random Walk Down Wall Street: The Time-Tested Strategy for Successful Investing* (1973) was born in Boston in 1932 and is a well-known American economist, investor, businessman, and writer. He started out as an analyst on Wall Street before quickly moving into academia, earning a PhD in economics at Princeton University before taking a post in the institution's economics department. Following a distinguished academic career at Princeton, he now holds the title of Chemical Bank Chairman's Professor of Economics Emeritus ("emeritus" means retired).

During his academic career, Malkiel was also active in the business world; he served as director for over a dozen private companies, in the US government as a member of the Council of Economic Advisers (a body that advises the US president), and as president of the American Finance Association.*

Despite all these professional achievements in the worlds of academia and business, Malkiel remains best known for his book *A Random Walk Down Wall Street*. It was first published in 1973 and became a bestseller. It has now run to 11 editions.

The publication of *A Random Walk* thrust Malkiel into the forefront of a debate over whether investment professionals can predict movements in the stock market. He has remained at the center of this debate ever since, publishing many other books and articles in the field of investment theory and practice. He has also created or supported real-life investment products (funds in which investors can put their money, and so on) in line with the conclusions of *A Random Walk*.

What Does *A Random Walk Down Wall Street* Say?

A Random Walk is a book about the stock market—principally the US stock market—which argues that stock prices move in completely random ways. This claim sets its author in instant opposition to the conventional wisdom of Wall Street and its many "experts" (a term that, in the context of financial services—banks, insurance companies, investment funds, and so on—Malkiel can only mock). These experts claim that they can predict the future performance—that is to say, price changes—of stock markets. *A Random Walk* argues directly, and forcefully, against this idea: "Short-run changes in stock prices are unpredictable. Investment advisory services, earnings forecasts, and complicated chart patterns are useless."[1]

In a way, this vision of market "randomness" is a compliment to Wall Street's efficiency.* There is such intense competition among those playing the stock market, Malkiel argues, that there is no real advantage to be gained. So many people are collecting and spreading information that could affect stock prices that there are no (legal) secrets left with which to exploit a "sure thing." Any secret is already out to everyone else, too—except in cases of insider trading* (buying or selling stocks based on confidential information, such as company plans to expand or, on the other hand, plans to announce poor earnings), which is illegal.

As a result, Malkiel claims that every current stock price captures all current available information about the value of the firm in question. This idea, the efficient market hypothesis* (EMH), is more popularly known as the random walk theory.*

The EMH assumes that whenever new information appears that would enable someone to gain a genuine "edge" (the ability to predict before other investors whether an individual stock will go up or down), it spreads to everyone quickly. No single party is able to benefit from it alone. An investor might (legally) receive a piece of news a split second before everyone else, and so make a brilliant investment as a result, but in the long term this is hardly a strategy that will keep working; this is because the stock market "is so good at adjusting to new information that no one can predict its future course in a superior manner. Because of the actions of the pros, the prices of individual stock quickly reflect all the news that is available."[2]

So how does someone invest his or her money, if each individual stock listed on the stock market is really a crapshoot (just a question of luck)?

One thing that seems certain is the total value of the stock market itself: over decades this has increased significantly, despite peaks and troughs (ups and downs) along the way. Malkiel recommends a "buy-and-hold" strategy of selecting a portfolio* (that is, basket) of stocks so varied that the performance of the whole portfolio of different stocks mirrors that of the stock market average. Over the long term, such an investment seems sure to make significant returns. If you cannot beat the market, it best to bet on it. In its way, this is a very radical statement—and the last thing Wall Street professionals want the "average" investor to do.

Why Does *A Random Walk Down Wall Street* Matter?

Malkiel's argument has shown remarkable staying power since it first appeared in 1973. For the public, *A Random Walk* provided an intellectual challenge to the value of professional money managers. Not only is it impossible for these managers to consistently beat the market, they also charge customers high fees and high transaction costs each time they buy or sell shares. As a result, even after 11 editions of the book, many professionals in the financial services industry still want to debunk its conclusions. Yet everyone with any interest in the stock market must confront its conclusions. Despite the hostility it has aroused, it has remained popular among investment professionals, financial theorists, and "average" investors. Winning a following among this last group is quite an achievement, since "average investors" are so frequently in the grip of investment gurus promising to help them "beat the market."

Through all 11 editions, Malkiel has maintained that *no one* can beat the market reliably over time. Data on the general performance of money managers versus the performance of the stock market itself supports his claim. So his argument is still as relevant as ever. More than four decades after it was first published, *A Random Walk* is still regularly cited, talked about in the financial press and among investment theory academics, and attacked by Wall Street professionals.

Students reading this text will engage with basic questions in the world of investment theory and practice: How and why do stock prices change? Can anyone really "beat the market"? If they cannot, what does this mean for the average investor? According to Malkiel, "There have been so many bewildering claims about the stock market that it's important to have a book that sets the record straight."[3]

It also provides financial know-how, even (or particularly) to the nonspecialist. Malkiel aims to provide "fundamentally a readable investment guide for individual investors."[4] The financial world has become much more sophisticated over the past 40 years. Investment funds now use a dizzying variety of financial instruments, which, technically speaking, can be any kind of tradable asset (including cash), but can even be things such as the debt held by companies or individuals. Malkiel's book is a clear, to-the-point guide through this often confusing world.

This book has remained popular—and hotly disputed—for over 40 years. Whether or not he is right, it is fair to say Malkiel has succeeded in his goals for *A Random Walk Down Wall Street*—he has made professionals and average investors alike take seriously the idea that you cannot beat the market.

NOTES

1   Burton G. Malkiel, *A Random Walk Down Wall Street: The Time-Tested Strategy for Successful Investing* (New York: W.W. Norton & Company, 2015), 26.

2   Malkiel, *Random Walk,* 190.

3   Malkiel, *Random Walk*, 18.

4   Malkiel, *Random Walk*, 19.

SECTION 1
INFLUENCES

MODULE 1
THE AUTHOR AND THE HISTORICAL CONTEXT

KEY POINTS

- *A Random Walk* bases its analysis on the efficient market hypothesis* (EMH), commonly known as the random walk theory,* according to which the movements of stock* prices are unpredictable.

- The book combines Malkiel's academic understanding of investment theory with his professional financial expertise.

- Challenging fashionable and often very expensive investment strategies, the EMH has provoked spirited debate—especially with investment professionals who make money by claiming they know how to beat the market.

Why Read This Text?

First published in 1973, Burton G. Malkiel's *A Random Walk Down Wall Street: The Time-Tested Strategy for Successful Investing* is now in its 11th edition, and 1.5 million copies have been sold. Promoting the efficient market hypothesis* (EMH)—the principle that the stock market is so efficient* (everything knowable about a company is reflected in its stock price) that future (unknowable) price movements cannot be predicted—it has become a classic in literature related to investment. Malkiel remains a leading figure in academic and financial communities. He still famously believes that "the market prices stocks so efficiently that a blindfolded monkey throwing darts at the stock listings can select a portfolio* that performs as well as those managed by the experts."[1] ("Portfolio" here refers to a basket of shares selected

> 66 I have been a lifelong investor and successful participant in the market. How successful I will not say, for it is a peculiarity of the academic world that a professor is not supposed to make money. 99
>
> Burton G. Malkiel, *A Random Walk Down Wall Street*

to bring a return to an investor.)

The EMH promoted in the book states that security* prices capture all available news and information about their individual companies. "Securities" are commonly things such as stocks or bonds: * financial contracts declaring some ownership of a publically traded corporation (stocks), or a promise of repayment for a loan from a corporation or a governmental body (bonds). If a share price does not reflect all available information, then these shares have been priced incorrectly (that is to say, inefficiently). According to the EMH, people will flock to exploit this imbalance (by either buying or selling the incorrectly priced stock) until this inefficiency disappears, and that process tends to happen almost instantly—so quickly that making money from exploiting such inefficiencies over the long term is more or less impossible.

In light of this theory, Malkiel proposes betting on the market itself: by diversifying an investment portfolio (the stocks held) among shares in a great number of companies, the value of the portfolio will match that of the whole stock market. This is called an "index fund,"* which has low operating expenses and low portfolio turnover—few fees paid to professionals and little buying and selling.[2] This incredibly simple strategy almost always outperforms the sophisticated mutual fund managers of Wall Street (the financial district of New York City, and the US money market more generally) over time.

When investors come together to own a diverse portfolio of stocks jointly, which is managed by investment professionals, they invest in "mutual funds."* Always seeking to maximize returns for themselves, mutual fund managers constantly buy and sell stocks for the portfolio—charging high fees and generating capital gains tax* (tax on the increase in the value of the shares) that is payable by their clients along the way.

Author's Life

Malkiel was born in Boston in 1932. He graduated from the prestigious Boston Latin School before attending Harvard University, gaining a BA in 1953 and an MBA in 1955. After serving in the Finance Corps of the US Army, Malkiel spent two years as an associate at the former Wall Street investment firm Smith Barney & Company (now part of Morgan Stanley Wealth Management).

In 1960, Malkiel moved from Wall Street to academia, earning a PhD in economics from Princeton University, one of the leading institutions in the United States. He became an assistant professor there, and quickly rose to a chaired professorship (the highest academic post) and head of the economics department. For Malkiel, this move into academia was key to unlocking better investment strategies.

The move cut him off from his former colleagues on Wall Street, who believe that "academics are so immersed in equations and Greek symbols (to say nothing of stuffy prose) that they couldn't tell a bull from a bear, even in a china shop"[3] (in the language of the stock market, "bulls" are optimistic that prices will rise; "bears" are pessimistic and expect prices to fall). Nonetheless Malkiel also served on the board of directors for a number of companies during this period.

This dual career in business and academia makes Malkiel quite an unusual (and unusually successful) figure. After becoming dean of Yale University's School of Organization and Management in 1981, he eventually returned to Princeton as the Chemical Bank Chairman's Professor of Economics, a post he now holds *in emeritus* (in retirement).

Author's Background

In *A Random Walk*, Malkiel asks a clearly focused question: Is the movement of any company's shares predictable, or are such movements completely random?

If security prices do indeed capture all available news and information about their individual companies, then the future paths of prices can only be random, since they depend entirely on future news: "If an item of news were not random, that is, if it were dependent on an earlier item of news, then it wouldn't be news at all."[4]

By straddling the world of business and academia, Malkiel has a privileged view of how each of these worlds works. Throughout *A Random Walk* he attacks both for obscuring (in his eyes) the simple truth about markets: that they obey the EMH, and that investing in the stock market is therefore a "random walk." In this sense, Malkiel's voice is unique in both the investment world and that of the academic community of investment theory and research.

Malkiel has certainly reached a huge audience in both worlds. The Vanguard Group,* a low-cost index fund investment group where Malkiel served as a director for almost 30 years, now manages over $3 trillion worth of assets. As Malkiel himself notes in *A Random Walk*, since the financial crash of 2007–8* (an event triggered by the collapse of the highly risky US housing market and the losses incurred by financial institutions that had invested in it), investors endorse his simple strategy more and more: "During 2014, about one-third of the money invested by individuals and institutions was invested in index funds. And that percentage continues to grow."[5]

Although he is now retired, Malkiel remains a productive academic.

NOTES

1   Burton G. Malkiel, *A Random Walk Down Wall Street: The Time-Tested Strategy for Successful Investing* (New York: W.W. Norton & Company, 2015), 19.

2   Malkiel, *Random Walk*, 383.

3   Malkiel, *Random Walk,* 26.

4   Malkiel, *Random Walk*, 155.

5   Malkiel, *Random Walk*, 181.

MODULE 2
ACADEMIC CONTEXT

KEY POINTS

- An academic examination of the stock market, *A Random Walk* considers whether or not its performance can be predicted.

- In the book, Malkiel challenged technical analysis* and fundamental analysis,* two leading approaches that claim to predict stock* price movements; he has continued to challenge newer approaches.

- A number of other economists have come to the same conclusions, both before and after Malkiel's book was published.

The Work in its Context

Burton G. Malkiel's *A Random Walk Down Wall Street: The Time-Tested Strategy for Successful Investing* introduces a new type of investment analysis called the efficient market hypothesis (EMH),* sometimes referred to as the random walk theory.* The text deals with one of the most basic questions in finance—why prices change in security* markets.[1] ("Securities" are things such as stocks and bonds.)* It states that a stock price captures all available information about the value of a firm, and because of this, there is no way to "beat the market" using legally available information.

Many investors try to take advantage of the gap that frequently exists between a stock's price and its actual value. They try to identify stocks that are undervalued, and expected to increase in value—especially those that will increase more than others.[2] This latter difference is key, because someone who picks stocks that perform

❝ Markets are not always or even usually correct. But NO ONE PERSON OR INSTITUTION CONSISTENTLY KNOWS MORE THAN THE MARKET. **❞**

Burton G. Malkiel, *A Random Walk Down Wall Street: The Time-Tested Strategy for Successful Investing*

better than others "beats the market." Investors often use a dizzying number of forecasting techniques to find such superior returns.[3] However, the EMH argues that such advantages cannot exist on a regular basis for anyone.

Few theories have created such passionate debate. The noted Harvard economist Michael Jensen* has said, for example, that "there is no other proposition in economics which has more solid empirical*[data-based] evidence supporting it than the efficient market hypothesis," while the famous investor Peter Lynch* has said "Efficient markets? That's a bunch of junk, crazy stuff."[4]

Overview of the Field

The field's basic question is whether there is any way to predict the movements of stock prices. This naturally invites an enormous number of opinions from both investors and academic investment theorists, with some arguing that stock prices are predictable while others are convinced that they are not.

The leading views on this subject come from two long-standing schools of thought: "technical analysis" and "fundamental analysis." Malkiel challenges them both.

In simple terms, technical analysis studies past stock prices and volumes of trading in order to predict future prices. For followers of this approach, the market is only 10 percent logical and 90 percent psychological;* they "view the investment game as one of anticipating how the other players will behave."[5]

Fundamental analysis, however, tries to do the opposite—it seeks to remain immune to the optimism and pessimism of the masses. This approach analyzes financial statistics, such as company earnings or asset values, to identify "undervalued" stocks.[6]

Since *A Random Walk* was first published, new schools of thought have emerged. Malkiel has kept pace with all these developments and often examines these new theories with serious academic research. He remains skeptical that any such approaches or "wizardry" can truly work and "beat the market."

Academic Influences

When the French mathematician Louis Bachelier* published *Théorie de la spéculation* (1900), he proclaimed that "the mathematical expectation of the speculator is zero." In other words, an investor who speculates or tries to guess which stocks will perform better cannot expect to make any profit, as losses will always equal gains. Far ahead of his time, Bachelier's study was largely ignored for more than five decades.[7] By the time it was rediscovered, theorists such as the British economist John Maynard Keynes* and the US economist Milton Friedman* had been addressing the same question and had come to similar conclusions.

In 1970, Eugene F. Fama,* an economist from the United States who went on to win a Nobel Prize in Economic Sciences, published a conclusive paper on the subject. In it he stated that "the evidence in support of the efficient market model is extensive, and (somewhat uniquely in economics) contradictory evidence is sparse."[8]

Along with such mathematical analyses, a growing literature of distrust about the competence of Wall Street professionals appeared. The US stockbroker Fred Schwed Jr.'s* book *Where Are the Customers' Yachts?* (1940) was an early classic of this genre: "Pitifully few financial experts have ever known for two years what was going to happen to any class of securities,"* Schwed wrote. "The majority are usually spectacularly wrong in a much shorter time than that."[9]

More recently, the Nobel Prize-winning economist Robert J. Shiller* published *Irrational Exuberance* (2003), criticizing the market's "positive feedback loops" where price rises encourage more people to buy, raising the price further, until a kind of Ponzi* scheme develops based on mass psychology* rather than fraud[10] (in a Ponzi scheme, early investors receive high rates of return, but when no more investors can be found to inject money, the fraudulent scheme collapses and most participants lose their money). The economist Nassim Nicholas Taleb's* *The Black Swan* (2007) casts empirical* and philosophical doubt on the belief that past stock performance can anticipate future performance.[11] (Empirical evidence is evidence that can be verified by observation.)

A Random Walk's conclusions place it in this tradition of critical financial literature, backed by Malkiel's serious and ongoing academic research.

NOTES

1   Jonathan Clarke, et al., "The Efficient Markets Hypothesis," in *Expert Financial Planning: Investment Strategies from Industry Leaders*, ed. Robert C. Arffa (New York: John Wiley & Sons, 2001), 126.

2   Clarke, "The Efficient Markets Hypothesis," 126.

3   Clarke, "The Efficient Markets Hypothesis," 126.

4   Clarke, "The Efficient Markets Hypothesis," 127.

5   Burton G. Malkiel, *A Random Walk Down Wall Street: The Time-Tested Strategy for Successful Investing* (New York: W.W. Norton & Company, 2015), 110.

6   Burton G. Malkiel, "The Efficient Market Hypothesis and Its Critics," *Journal of Economic Perspectives* 17, no. 1 (winter, 2003): 59.

7   Martin Sewell, "History of the Efficient Market Hypothesis," *UCL Research Note* 11, no. 4 (2011): 2.

8 Eugene F. Fama, "Efficient Markets: A Review of Theory and Empirical Work," *The Journal of Finance* 25, no. 2 (May 1970): 383.

9 Fred Schwed Jr., *Where Are the Customers' Yachts?* (Hoboken: John Wiley & Sons, 2006), 14.

10 Robert J. Shiller, *Irrational Exuberance* (Princeton: Princeton University Press, 2000), 64–8.

11 Nassim Nicholas Taleb, *The Black Swan: The Impact of the Highly Improbable* (London: Penguin, 2007).

MODULE 3
THE PROBLEM

KEY POINTS

- The modern idea of an "efficient* market" as applied to stock* exchanges first appeared in a 1965 article published by the US economist Eugene F. Fama.* A radical idea at the time, it challenged the whole value of the financial services industry* and inspired Malkiel to write his book.

- The efficient market hypothesis* (EMH) is opposed by various theories that try to find and exploit patterns in stock price changes.

- The financial collapse of 2007–8* was perhaps the biggest challenge to the EMH, with some claiming it disproves the hypothesis.

Core Question

The central questions Burton G. Malkiel asks in *A Random Walk Down Wall Street: The Time-Tested Strategy for Successful Investing* are, "Why do stock prices change? How do those changes take place? And is it possible to predict them?" Indeed, these questions are some of the most central to the field of finance altogether.

While on the surface these sound like rational and mathematical problems, the role of emotion in stock markets—particularly the extremes of greed and panic—is not to be underestimated. The British economist John Maynard Keynes* famously said the stock market's movements are due to quirky psychological* factors: "A large proportion of our positive activities depend on spontaneous optimism rather than mathematical expectations," he said.[1] They are dependent on what he called "animal spirits—a spontaneous urge to action rather

66 A blindfolded monkey throwing darts at the stock listings could select a portfolio that would do just as well as one selected by the experts. **99**

Burton G. Malkiel, *A Random Walk Down Wall Street*

than inaction."[2] Keynes's conclusion was that "there is nothing so disastrous as a rational investment policy in an irrational world."[3]

The question as to how and why stock prices move remains crucial, and it has a huge impact on both the investor and the entire financial services industry. The end of World War II* in 1945 brought a new era of American economic prosperity, as record amounts of money were invested in the stock market. As a result, the financial sector grew rapidly, with financial professionals all promising superior returns (an obvious impossibility, since it impossible for all to be above average). Since then, there have been numerous, well-known strategies that have all promised to anticipate "what will happen next" on the stock market.

The term "efficient market" first appeared in a 1965 article by Eugene F. Fama,* where he proposed that, "In an efficient market at any point in time the actual price of a security will be a good estimate of its intrinsic (real, core) value."[4] Supporters of EMH insist there is absolutely no way for stock price movements to be predicted. Yet this was a radical idea, prompting Malkiel to write his book challenging the financial services industry and its many claims to almost clairvoyant, far-sighted analyses of stock price movements.

The Participants

If stock price movements are driven by some mysterious mixture of logic and emotion, it is perhaps not surprising that the two biggest forecasting camps focus on one side or the other, almost exclusively.

Technical analysts* study past price movements to forecast future ones. They look for any patterns in price movements, based on the idea that the emotional or psychological side of investing, rather than the logical side, drives such shifts. It is a game of studying how other investors in the market behave, in order to anticipate what the crowd will probably do in the future.[5] By contrast, fundamental analysts* try to discover what a stock is really worth, its "true value," in order to exploit the gap between any (inefficiently) low price and a stock's higher true value. Together, these two schools make up a large part of the financial services industry.

Over time, more rivals to the EMH have appeared. Perhaps surprisingly, these have come from within the academic community rather than the business world. One rival is modern portfolio theory.* This states that portfolios* of relatively risky stocks can be made much less risky if they are diversified (mixed with other stocks) in the correct way. Another rival, behavioral finance,* has become a rapidly evolving field. It holds that investors are far from rational; it studies behavior such as overconfidence, biased judgments, and herd mentality. The idea is that insights into these factors can enable investors to make money from the gaps they create between stock prices and their true value.

Numerous other financial investment strategies continue to spring up, and many gain huge followings.

The Contemporary Debate

The EMH is more than an idea; intellectually speaking, it is a threat to much of the financial services industry. If it is impossible to beat the market, then why even try?—especially given the high management fees, transaction fees for each purchase or sale of stocks, and the relatively high capital gains tax that becomes payable on any stocks sold for a profit.

Fama's highly regarded research paper "Efficient Capital Markets:

A Review of Theory and Empirical Work" (1970) backed the EMH with much real-world research. During the following decade, this model continued to hold sway among investors and economists. It dominated both financial and academic circles, which produced a steady stream of published research to support it.[6] However, in the 1980s and 1990s, the EMH began to be questioned by both academics and the business world. For example, research showed that investors regularly overreact or underreact to news—meaning they bid too high or too low for stocks. This alone, at least partially, disproves the EMH.[7]

The economic crash of 2007–8 was perhaps the greatest challenge to the EMH. Many, including the billionaire hedge-fund manager George Soros,* saw the crisis as having discredited the EMH. After all, certain financial products, in particular those tied to the US subprime real estate market* (risky investments in the housing market) were priced way too high, buoyed by investors' continued decisions to buy in search of high profits. In the end, the bubble*—gross overpricing—burst, and most of those investments became all but worthless.

Addressing the 2007–8 housing crash head-on, Malkiel says the EMH had indeed worked; the markets ended up finding the correct price for these investments. It just took several years to happen. "The clear conclusion," insists Malkiel, "is that, in every case, the market did correct itself. The market eventually corrects any irrationality."[8]

NOTES

1　John Maynard Keynes, *The General Theory of Employment, Interest and Money* (London: Macmillan, 1936), 161–2.

2　Keynes, *The General Theory*, 161–2.

3　Milton Friedman and Anna Jacobson Schwartz, *A Monetary History of the United States, 1867–1960* (Princeton: Princeton University Press, 1963), 814.

4   Eugene F. Fama, "Efficient Markets: A Review of Theory and Empirical Work," *The Journal of Finance* 25, no. 2 (May 1970): 383.

5   Burton G. Malkiel, *A Random Walk Down Wall Street: The Time-Tested Strategy for Successful Investing* (New York: W.W. Norton & Company, 2015), 110–1.

6   Ramy Majouji, "The Financial Markets Context," Open University OpenLearn, accessed November 10, 2015, http://www.open.edu/openlearn/money-management/money/accounting-and-finance/the-financial-markets-context/content-section—acknowledgements.

7   Majouji, "The Financial Markets Context."

8   Malkiel, *Random Walk*, 104.

MODULE 4
THE AUTHOR'S CONTRIBUTION

KEY POINTS

- In *A Random Walk,* Malkiel presents much evidence and actual trading data to demolish the various investing theories that claim they can perform better than the stock* market average.

- By translating the theoretical efficient market hypothesis* (EMH) into a real-life investment strategy—by promoting index funds,* which bet on the rise in the value of the market as a whole rather on the value of individual shares—Malkiel influenced the world of investing as few others have.

- Although largely developed by other academics such as the Nobel Prize-winning economist Eugene F. Fama,* Malkiel took the theory further and popularized it.

Author's Aims

Burton G. Malkiel's aims in writing *A Random Walk Down Wall Street: The Time-Tested Strategy for Successful Investing* were admirably simple. First, he wanted to prove the validity of the efficient market hypothesis (EMH), which states that prices of securities* (like stocks and bonds*) capture all available news and information about the companies that issue them. He has a wealth of data and evidence, including stock prices over time, that he elegantly presents. Malkiel then aims to disprove the challengers to the EMH, one by one, particularly the long-standing schools of technical analysis* and fundamental analysis.* He also aims to disprove newer, fashionable investment strategies such as modern portfolio theory* (an approach in which investors minimize risks by choosing assets whose risks offset each other) and,

> **❝** I am not promising you stock-market miracles. Indeed, a subtitle for this book might well have been *The Get Rich Slowly but Surely Book.* **❞**
>
> Burton G. Malkiel, *A Random Walk Down Wall Street*

despite acknowledging the valuable insights it has produced, is generally critical of the growing academic field of behavioral finance*(which explores the psychological* characteristics of market participants to explain market movements). "Imagine," he says, "a whole new field in which to publish papers, give lectures for hefty fees, and write graduate theses."[1]

Malkiel aims to show that after taking into account the heavy fees, transaction costs, and tax burdens that come with all "actively managed" strategies (strategies based on frequently buying and selling stocks), the average investor is much better off simply betting on the market itself by investing in an index fund made up of a variety of stocks and then waiting. An index fund is a portfolio* of diverse stocks, selected to allow its performance to mirror that of the overall stock market.

Finally, Malkiel aims to provide a full financial guide to his reader. *A Random Walk* offers a broad range of financial advice useful to the average investor, ranging from insurance, to paying for a child's education, to (legal) tax avoidance.

Approach

While the economist Eugene F. Fama is often thought of as the father of the EMH, *A Random Walk* presented these academic findings to the nonspecialist reader. When the book was published (1973), a general awareness was growing that most "actively managed" mutual funds* (money pooled by a number of investors and managed by professionals who buy and sell securities on behalf of those investors) were not performing better than the stock market itself. Malkiel cited the theoretical EMH to make an appeal in *A Random Walk's* first edition: "What we need is a … minimum management-fee mutual fund [in which the investor is not charged for buying and selling shares] that simply buys the hundreds of stocks making up the broad stock-market averages and does no trading from security to security in an attempt to catch the winners."[2] He called, in other words, for an "index mutual fund": a portfolio of stocks so diverse that it performs similarly to the overall stock market.

Through the EMH, *A Random Walk* calls for a very practical, long-term approach that was already being followed elsewhere. The market theorist John Bogle* founded the US investment management company the Vanguard Group* the year after *A Random Walk's* publication, and in 1976 created the world's first index mutual fund that was available to the regular investor. While Bogle had many inspirations for this revolutionary index fund, and had long been interested in this approach, it was Malkiel and *A Random Walk* that voiced its goals most clearly to the general public. In 1977, Malkiel himself joined the board of directors of the Vanguard Group, where he served for 28 years. This group is now one of the largest mutual fund companies in the world, with over $3 trillion in total assets under management. While Vanguard's pioneering index fund was widely mocked when it started in 1974 for not even *trying* to beat the market, index mutual funds are now considered to be the industry standard. *A Random Walk* became the popular intellectual justification for the growth of such funds.

Contribution in Context

When Fama published his groundbreaking paper "Efficient Capital Markets: A Review of Theory and Empirical Work" in 1970, his research confirmed what many others had been thinking for some time.[3] At Princeton University, for example, Bogle's thesis title had been "Mutual Funds can make no claims to superiority over the Market Averages" (1951). Other influential studies closely followed the publication of *A Random Walk* in 1973. The influential economist Paul A. Samuelson's* 1974 paper "Challenge to Judgment," for example, famously declared that "superior investment performance is unproved."[4] The US investment consultant Charles D. Ellis's* 1975 article "The Loser's Game" reached a similar conclusion: "The investment management business (it should be a profession but is not) is built upon a simple and basic belief: Professional money managers can beat the market. That premise appears to be false."[5] Like Malkiel, Ellis recommends an indexed fund and an acceptance by investors that the market average is the best they can hope for in the stock market as "If you can't beat the market, you certainly should consider joining it."[6]

Even if Malkiel's views in *A Random Walk* were not original or unique at the time, his key contribution to the field still cannot be overestimated. Few theorists have made a bigger impact in the world of investment; his book made the ideas so much more popular on a wide scale, changing the investment world and helping to invent a new type of mutual fund. The debate it has inspired about "beating the market" has continued for over 40 years.[7]

NOTES

1   Burton G. Malkiel, *A Random Walk Down Wall Street: The Time-Tested Strategy for Successful Investing,* (New York: W.W. Norton & Company, 2015), 230.

2   Malkiel, *Random Walk*, 226–7.

3   Eugene F. Fama, "Efficient Markets: A Review of Theory and Empirical Work," *The Journal of Finance* 25, no. 2 (May 1970).

4   Paul A. Samuelson, "Challenge to Judgment," *The Journal of Portfolio Management* 1, no. 1 (1974): 17.

5   Charles D. Ellis, "The Loser's Game," *The Financial Analysts Journal* 31, no. 4 (July/August 1975): 19.

6   Ellis, "The Loser's Game," 26.

7   The Motley Fool, "Investment Greats: Burton Malkiel," accessed November 21, 2015, http://news.fool.co.uk/news/investing/2011/01/04/investment-greats-burton-malkiel.aspx.

SECTION 2
IDEAS

MODULE 5
MAIN IDEAS

KEY POINTS

- Malkiel has two key themes in *A Random Walk:* the efficient market hypothesis (EMH),* and the "smart" way to invest by betting on the stock market as a whole rather than on individual stocks.*

- The book uses data to show that a broad-based index fund,* reflecting the value of the stock market as a whole, has historically performed better than any other strategy for stock market investing.

- Malkiel uses straightforward and accessible language to argue forcefully why his investment approach is better than speculating*—roughly, betting—on short-term profits.

Key Themes

There are two main themes that run through Burton G. Malkiel's *A Random Walk Down Wall Street: The Time-Tested Strategy for Successful Investing.* The first is the efficient market hypothesis; the second is the key distinction between "speculation" and "investment."

According to the random walk theory,* stock prices move in completely unpredictable ways. The market rests on the efficient market hypothesis, being "so efficient—prices move so quickly when information arises—that no one can buy or sell fast enough to benefit. And real news develops randomly, that is, unpredictably."[1] The investor's central question then arises: How can you estimate a stock's "true value" to ensure that you do not overpay when buying shares, or how can you buy something undervalued so that you can "beat the market?"[2]

As Malkiel puts it bluntly many times: this is impossible. No

> **❝** Anomalies can crop up, markets can get irrationally
> optimistic, and often they attract unwary investors.
> But, eventually, true value is recognized by the market,
> and this is the main lesson investors must heed. **❞**
>
> Burton G. Malkiel, *A Random Walk Down Wall Street*

investor can beat the market over the long term, as "The odds of
selecting superior stocks or anticipating the general direction of the
market are even. Your guess is as good as that of the ape, your
stockbroker, or even mine."[3]

Once this fact (in Malkiel's eyes, at least) is agreed, the true
"investor" can use the EMH to invest his or her money wisely. This is
done by simply betting on the market itself through a broad-based
index fund (a fund that buys a wide variety of stocks and then keeps
them). That way, the returns on an investment mirror those of the
stock market as a whole over the long term, which practically
guarantees major gains. Only the foolish "speculator" continues to aim
for superior returns in the short term. As the market is a "random
walk," this is impossible to keep up—something the EMH makes
obvious, but which those working in the investment business will
always deny (for obviously self-interested reasons: to protect the fees
they earn managing people's money, having promised them earnings
higher than the average increase in stock value).

Exploring the Ideas

A Random Walk argues that the EMH holds true in real stock markets,
including the New York stock exchange.* If this were not true, it
would be much easier to "beat the market," but Malkiel shows
convincingly how difficult this would be to achieve: "An investor
with $10,000 at the start of 1969 who invested in a Standard & Poor's

500-Stock Index Fund would have had a portfolio worth $736,196 by June 2014, assuming that all dividends were reinvested. A second investor who instead purchased shares in the average actively managed fund would have seen his investment grow to $501,470. The difference is dramatic."[4]

That is to say, the index fund, which invests broadly and in accordance with the EMH (it simply buys shares in a wide variety of companies) does almost 1.5 times as well as the fund managed by "expert" investment managers. This timespan includes many "up" and "down" years for the stock market, but over the long term the index mutual fund still does much better. These figures clearly show that, given enough time, Wall Street is able to deliver on its promises, and point toward a smarter way of investing. So why don't more people simply put their money into a long-term index mutual fund? The answer is that many people are more interested in "speculating" than "investing," a key difference made in *A Random Walk*.

An investor, in Malkiel's eyes, "buys stocks likely to produce a dependable future stream of cash returns and capital gains when measured over years or decades."[5] In contrast, Malkiel has little time for the speculator, who "buys stocks hoping for a short-term gain over the next few days or weeks."[6] Malkiel argues against such speculation, which often buys into the momentum of rising stocks to make a quick profit. He calls this the "Madness of Crowds." Starting with the Tulip Bulb Craze* in sixteenth-century Holland (when competition pushed up the price of tulip bulbs to astronomical levels, a situation that was soon followed by a price collapse), Malkiel summarizes a series of similar "bubbles"* that eventually proved disastrous for investors who bought into them. His point remains clear throughout: "Invariably, the hottest stocks or fund in one period are the worst performers in the next."[7] The very common desire to get rich quick makes such speculators easy prey for Wall Street's promises of "market-beating" strategies. In a way, Malkiel completely agrees with the financial fraudster Charles Ponzi* (creator of the Ponzi scheme,* where high rates of return are promised to investors, which are paid out from the money provided by new investors) who once said that "When a man's vision is fixed on one thing, he might as well be blind."[8]

Malkiel then reviews many different forms of these active investment strategies ("active" in that they involve buying and selling stocks much more often than in the passive approach he advocates) that still claim to "beat the market." They include technical analysis* (which examines past price trends to predict future ones) and fundamental analysis* (which seeks to find the "true value" of a stock). He also examines modern portfolio theory,* which tries to balance risky stocks against each other, and the new field of behavioral finance,* which examines the psychological* side to investing (like "herd behavior"—the influence of mass psychology). Malkiel finds some insights in this relatively new field, though he views them as being quite limited.

Malkiel's conclusion is clear and consistent: "The core of every investment portfolio should consist of low-cost, tax-efficient, broad-based index funds," which guarantee market return.[9]

Language and Expression

Malkiel aims to provide the reader with an easily accessible guide to investment and finance, including discussion of academic advances in investment theory and practice.[10] He matches his insights into complex investment models with clear explanations. His style is conversational, informal, friendly, and at times even humorous. For example, at one point he states that, "If your broker calls to say that IPO (initial public offering*) shares will be available for you, you can bet that the new issue is a dog"[11]—that is, not especially valuable. Sometimes, however, he adopts a more professorial tone that some might find off-putting, or even patronizing. For example, he writes at one point that "[t]he conscientious reader will now note that in the schematic illustration…" before presenting the reader with information.[12]

What often makes Malkiel's ideas so strong is not their originality so much as the way he expresses them. Simple points, like the importance of not panicking and selling shares when their prices fall unexpectedly, have a big impact in Malkiel's hands: "A buy-and-hold investor would have seen one dollar invested in the Dow Jones Industrial Average* [an average of 30 stocks traded on the New York stock exchange*] in 1900 grow to \$290 by the start of 2013. Had that investor missed the best five days each year, however, that dollar investment would have been worth less than a penny in 2013."[13]

NOTES

1   Burton G. Malkiel, *A Random Walk Down Wall Street: The Time-Tested Strategy for Successful Investing* (New York: W.W. Norton & Company, 2015), 184.

2   Malkiel, *Random Walk*, 105.

3   Malkiel, *Random Walk*, 190.

4   Malkiel, *Random Walk*, 17.

5   Malkiel, *Random Walk*, 28.

6   Malkiel, *Random Walk*, 28.

7   Malkiel, *Random Walk*, 254.

8   Douglas H. Dunn, *Ponzi* (New York: McGraw-Hill, 1975), 134.

9   Malkiel, *Random Walk*, 261.

10 Malkiel, *Random Walk*, 18.

11 Malkiel, *Random Walk*, 257.

12 Malkiel, *Random Walk*, 214.

13 Malkiel, *Random Walk*, 157.

MODULE 6
SECONDARY IDEAS

KEY POINTS

- Malkiel examines "new investment technology"—theories and strategies of investment—in some detail; but he is not convinced of their usefulness.

- Increased risk cannot be managed by diversification (buying a spread of different stocks* to create a diverse portfolio)* given the "systemic risks"* that Malkiel explores.

- Some big questions are left unanswered by Malkiel, such as what would happen if another asset bubble,* such as the one that caused the financial crash of 2007–8,* should burst: could the stock market itself survive it?

Other Ideas

The 11th edition of Burton G. Malkiel's *A Random Walk Down Wall Street: The Time-Tested Strategy for Successful Investing* gives "technical"* and "fundamental"* analyses short shrift before moving on to newer trends. He gives a thorough examination of what he sarcastically calls "the rarified world of 'new investment technology' created within the towers of the academy" and often followed today in the world of investment.[1]

Among the newer trends, Malkiel first explores modern portfolio theory,* which tries to balance risk in an overall portfolio* to produce superior returns. He also examines the "capital-asset pricing model," which basically claims that you *must* increase the total level of risk in a portfolio to earn superior returns. To do this in "the right way" requires following a method mysteriously labeled "beta."[2] The mathematical calculation for "beta" in a stock captures the sensitivity

> **❝ In investing, we are often our worst enemy. ❞**
> Burton G. Malkiel, *A Random Walk Down Wall Street*

of its price to general market movements.

Malkiel also reviews behavioral finance.* This approach studies irrational market behavior, including biased judgments, herd mentality, overconfidence, and loss aversion (a desire to avoid losses) in order to make money from the gaps these behaviors create between stock prices and their actual value. Despite finding much to fault in this model, Malkiel draws many insights from it that further inform his own "random walk" model.*

Finally, Malkiel provides a "Practical Guide for Random Walkers and Other Investors" that shows how to put his random walk model to work in all aspects of your personal finances.

Exploring the Ideas

Modern portfolio theory attempts to combine various riskier—and potentially higher-earning—stocks in ways that balance these risks against each other. For example, someone interested in an island economy might invest in both a large beach resort and an umbrella manufacturer in order to make money no matter what the island's weather.[3] The problem, according to Malkiel, is that the fortunes of most companies tend to move in the same direction. "When there is a recession and people are unemployed, they may buy neither summer vacations nor umbrellas. Therefore, one shouldn't expect in practice to get the neat kind of risk elimination just shown."[4]

This holds true in events such as the global economic recession of 2007–9,* when all markets fell at the same time. Those holding the riskiest stocks experienced the worst losses, no matter how they had been combined. This prompted Malkiel to comment, "Small wonder that some investors came to believe that diversification no longer seemed to be effective as a strategy against risk."[5]

Investors have invented a number of "smart beta"* strategies (mathematical formulas that try to capture market inefficiencies), which in general means trying to achieve higher returns with no increased risk.[6] Malkiel doubts the value of any of these strategies, writing, "Despite the mathematical manipulations involved, the basic idea behind the beta measurement is one of putting some precise numbers on the subjective feelings money managers have had for years." In other words, complex math is actually being used to support "hunches" or general opinions gleaned from far less objective sources.[7]

Again, Malkiel finds that this theory falls apart on the rocks of "systemic risk"—the tendency for all stocks to go along with the general market.[8] As in his discussion of modern portfolio theory, he shows that such systemic risk (that is, the risk that the whole market will drop in value) "cannot be eliminated by diversification" (spreading the risk by buying a suite of shares, for example). He also uses this logic to dismiss all models that try to determine the core value of different shares ("capital-asset pricing models,") which may be different from the price at which they are trading. This is because even if such a "pricing inefficiency" is discovered (that is, share prices do not reflect the real value of a company), they are sure to be corrected almost instantly as other investors observe the same thing: "Investors would snap at the chance to have these higher returns, bidding up the prices of stocks" that the models had correctly identified as being underpriced.[9]

Regarding behavioral finance, Malkiel disagrees completely with its belief that irrational behavior can lead to share prices that are too high or too low. "Efficient-market theory believers assert that smart rational traders will correct any mispricings that might arise from the presence of irrational traders."[10] Malkiel also admits that the insights of behavioral finance can help the average investor "quite a bit."[11]

Learning about these disruptive, irrational dynamics is a good thing for any investor (even if the all-knowing market will eventually weed them out).

Overlooked

Much academic literature supports Malkiel's EMH. As Malkiel says repeatedly in *A Random Walk*, asset bubbles (a term describing the increase in price of a stock or other asset beyond its actual value) must eventually be self-correcting. Investors will realize that prices cannot go any higher, and then a massive sell-off will take place. This abrupt sale will then cause the collapse of a company's share price and bring it down closer to its actual value.

However, Malkiel never addresses whether the market itself is strong enough to deal with these ever-bigger crashes. When bubbles burst on the scale of the 2007–8 subprime mortgage crisis* (a financial crisis founded on the trading of risky mortgages in the United States), government bailouts were required to preserve the very existence of the stock market. It is a clear and present danger that these crashes are getting bigger over time, rather than being isolated catastrophes. For example, the global financial meltdown of 2007–8 can be seen as "just the most recent installment in a recurrent pattern of financial overreach, taxpayer bailout, and subsequent Wall Street ingratitude. And all indications are that the pattern is set to continue."[12]

It is not absurd to suggest that a crash will occur of such size that the government will not be able to bail out the stock market, and investors will lose everything—even those "wise" investors who put their money in broad-based index funds, but Malkiel never addresses this possibility.

NOTES

1   Burton G. Malkiel, *A Random Walk Down Wall Street: The Time-Tested Strategy for Successful Investing* (New York: W.W. Norton & Company, 2015), 189.

2   Malkiel, *Random Walk*, 210.

3   Malkiel, *Random Walk*, 197–9.

4   Malkiel, *Random Walk*, 199.

5   Malkiel, *Random Walk*, 204.

6   Malkiel, *Random Walk,* 260–1.

7   Malkiel, *Random Walk*, 210.

8   Malkiel, *Random Walk*, 210.

9   Malkiel, *Random Walk*, 215.

10 Malkiel, *Random Walk*, 230.

11 Malkiel, *Random Walk*, 230.

12 Paul Krugman and Robin Wells, "The Busts Keep Getting Bigger: Why?" *The New York Review of Books*, July 14, 2011, accessed February 16, 2016, http://www.nybooks.com/articles/2011/07/14/busts-keep-getting-bigger-why/.

MODULE 7
ACHIEVEMENT

KEY POINTS

- In promoting the efficient market hypothesis* (EMH), Malkiel argued that almost every aspect of the conventional wisdom of the world of investment is nonsense. Readers and investors have responded positively to his message for over 40 years.

- *A Random Walk* put together and further developed a number of trends in investment theory from the early 1970s, mainly those based around the EMH.

- The 2007–8 financial crash* challenged Malkiel's approach; while critics say the price bubble* linked to the housing market shows the market had not found the right price for those assets, Malkiel says the model worked—it just took a few years for the bubble to burst before prices returned to the right level.

Assessing the Argument

When writing *A Random Walk Down Wall Street: The Time-Tested Strategy for Successful Investing*, Burton G. Malkiel's intention was clear: "There have been so many bewildering claims about the stock market that it's important to have a book that sets the record straight."[1] In this context, "setting the record straight" means accepting the idea that stock market prices reflect all currently available information about the stocks. The patterns of a stock's* past price movements will tell you nothing about its future movements, and the "true value" of a stock at any given time is always an estimate and never precise. Only the market (over time) reveals which stocks have a growing core value (as reflected by a rising price), and which do not.

❝ Talk to 10 money experts and you're likely to hear 10 recommendations for Burton Malkiel's classic investing book. ❞
Andrea Coombes, *The Wall Street Journal*

These ideas were born both from trends in investment theory in the late 1960s to early 1970s and the efficient market hypothesis (EMH). They have proved remarkably durable since then, as has the popularity of *A Random Walk*. The preface to the 11th edition of 2015 reflects just how solidly Malkiel's analysis has stood up to a rapidly changing world; the long list of things that did not exist when the first edition was published in 1973 includes everyday features of the financial landscape such as automatic teller machines, a number of modern trading techniques, mutual funds,* and tax-exempt funds— "to mention just a few of the changes that have occurred in the financial environment."[2]

Nonetheless, in this new world of complicated investment strategies, Malkiel remains certain about the EMH: "Now, over forty years later, I believe even more strongly in that original thesis."[3]

This statement is still both popular and credible—and taken as gospel by investors with trillions of dollars invested in broad-based index mutual funds.* It is a reflection of Malkiel's extraordinary achievement.

Achievement in Context
A Random Walk was first published in 1973 and addressed an entirely different era on Wall Street: one in which the EMH had recently been proved true by empirical* (data-based) evidence (as expressed in Eugene F. Fama's* landmark 1970 article "Efficient Markets: A Review of Theory and Empirical Work.")[4] The EMH was becoming generally accepted among investment theorists. Likewise, in the real-

life investment community the EMH and its implications were gaining ground: John Bogle* founded the Vanguard Group in 1974 and offered the first index mutual fund soon after. Malkiel's book was a central part of this movement, and made these ideas accessible to the nonspecialist, "average" investor.

Over the past 42 years Malkiel has regularly updated *A Random Walk*, with the new editions addressing new investment theories and practices. Meanwhile, an increasing number of academics and investors have challenged Malkiel's conclusions, creating a lively dialogue between those who still believe they can "actively" manage money to "beat the market," and voices like Malkiel who believe in the "passive" strategy of long-term investment in an index mutual fund.[5] However, the financial crash of 2007–8 in which the housing and stock markets collapsed—the worst crisis since the Great Depression* of the 1920s and 1930s—has perhaps produced new evidence that discredits the EMH on theoretical and practical grounds. This remains an ongoing debate.

Limitations

A Random Walk remains famous in the world of investment theory and practice and, as academics have increasingly questioned the random walk model,* Malkiel has remained its most vocal defender. In 2003, he wrote that "By the start of the twenty-first century, the intellectual dominance of the efficient market hypothesis had become far less universal. Many financial economists and statisticians began to believe that stock prices are at least partially predictable."[6]

Malkiel accepts that because of irrational or mistaken judgment by investors, "pricing irregularities and even predictable patterns in stock returns can appear over time and even persist for short periods." Yet he does not think such inefficiencies can last for any length of time—certainly not long enough to provide investors with a strategy for obtaining superior returns.[7]

The crash of 2007–8 provides a tough test for the EMH. For several years leading up to the crash, banks and other financial companies had been creating and selling various securities* based on housing mortgages. The prices of these investment instruments continued to rise until the crash, when many lost most or all of their value. Yet, in an "efficient" market, how could these assets have been so dramatically overpriced? Many felt the crash made the EMH obsolete because "the markets didn't work."[8] For Malkiel, this skepticism simply showed a misunderstanding of the EMH: "What the efficient market hypothesis does not mean is that markets are always correct," he said in a 2012 television interview, with reference to the crash.[9] "Markets are always wrong. The point is nobody knows at any one time—the price is wrong, but nobody knows whether it's too high or too low and the market is unbeatable, but that doesn't mean it's right."[10]

For Malkiel, the market only "gets it right" over the long term: once the bubble burst in 2007–8, assets and share prices went back down to a closer approximation of their real value. Once again, the fact that bubbles *do* burst is strong evidence, in Malkiel's eyes, that the EMH holds true.

Ultimately, *A Random Walk* depends on empirical data (records of actual trading prices, rather than theories) from stock markets. If the data cease to back up the EMH, then the text will find itself disproven. So far the EMH has held true over the long term. However, it is much more limited in the short or medium term—or when violent fluctuations occur, like the 2007–8 crash, which can threaten the entire financial system.

NOTES

1   Burton G. Malkiel, *A Random Walk Down Wall Street: The Time-Tested Strategy for Successful Investing* (New York: W.W. Norton & Company, 2015), 18.

2   Malkiel, *Random Walk*, 18.

3   Malkiel, *Random Walk*, 17.

4   Ramy Majouji, "The Financial Markets Context," Open University OpenLearn, accessed February 16, 2016, http://www.open.edu/openlearn/money-management/money/accounting-and-finance/the-financial-markets-context/content-section--acknowledgements.

5   Malkiel, *Random Walk*, 254.

6   Burton G. Malkiel, "The Efficient Market Hypothesis and its Critics," *Journal of Economic Perspectives* 17, no. 1 (2003): 60.

7   Malkiel, "The Efficient Market Hypothesis and its Critics," 80.

8   Sam Ro, "Finance Wizard Burton Malkiel Defends the Efficient Market Hypothesis," accessed November 25, 2015, http://www.businessinsider.com/burton-malkiel-efficient-market-hypothesis-2012-4?IR=T.

9   Ro, "Finance Wizard Burton Malkiel."

10 Ro, "Finance Wizard Burton Malkiel."

MODULE 8
PLACE IN THE AUTHOR'S WORK

KEY POINTS

- Malkiel's primary focus throughout his life's work has been the efficient market hypothesis* (EMH), or random walk theory,* and how to apply it to real-life stock* markets.

- For Malkiel, the "closed-end fund,"* which raises its capital only once by issuing a fixed number of shares, is the only type of actively traded fund that might reward investment.

- Although Malkiel has written many other books on different aspects of investment theory and practice, *A Random Walk* remains by far the best known and most studied.

Positioning

By the time *A Random Walk Down Wall Street: The Time-Tested Strategy for Successful Investing* was published in 1973, Burton G. Malkiel was already a leading American academic, with a professorship in economics at Princeton University. He had published books on international monetary policy, interest rate structures, and securities* options as well as a great number of influential articles. Nonetheless, *A Random Walk* became the high point of his career, and was soon a national best seller. It remains one of the most talked-about and debated texts in both academia and the professional financial services community.

A Random Walk is also an ongoing achievement: Malkiel has published 11 editions of the book, each largely different from those that came before. Every new edition has addressed the latest theories challenging the EMH, as well as new, more practical challenges from the day's business landscape. Accordingly, the heart of each edition has

> **❝** One of the most rewarding features for me in writing eleven editions of this book has been the many letters I have received from grateful investors. They tell me how much they have benefited from following the simple advice that has remained the same for forty years. Those timeless lessons involve broad diversification, annual rebalancing, using index funds, and staying the course. **❞**
>
> Burton G. Malkiel, *A Random Walk Down Wall Street*

remained essentially the same, both in its theoretical conclusion—that the EMH holds—and its investment advice—guiding the reader towards broad-based index mutual funds.* While the 2007–8 crash* and the global economic recession* have damaged the reputation of many investment strategies, Malkiel's approach in *A Random Walk* has been strengthened: investors can only be protected from such shocks by focusing on the long term.

Integration

Malkiel has had a remarkably varied career as both an academic and professional investment advisor. Since 1973 he has not only published 10 further editions of *A Random Walk*, but also a great number of other books and articles on different aspects of investing: how endowed institutions should manage risk (these are colleges or other nonprofit bodies in possession of a sum of donated money, known as an endowment. Generally only the interest earned from the endowment may be spent); beating inflation as an investor; and the structure of share prices, to name just a few.

Malkiel's main message in *A Random Walk* is that the best investment strategy is generally to place money in an index mutual fund*—a fund that pools the money of numerous investors and then buys stocks from a wide range of companies and holds on to them for a long time, so achieving the same long-term growth in value as the stock market as a whole. This buy-and-hold—or "passive"—investing approach also involves lower management fees than a mutual fund, which uses an "active" approach of frequent buying and selling in search of short-term profits.

While Malkiel generally disapproves of active investing, he makes an exception for one type: the "closed-end fund."[1] This preference emerged in his influential 1977 article "The Valuation of Closed-End Investment Company Shares," where he explores the opportunities presented by these unique funds.

Closed-end funds are actively managed, like mutual funds, but are structured entirely differently, and in a way that appeals to Malkiel despite being a departure from his usual exhortations for the passive-fund strategy. While most mutual funds can take on an increasing number of investors, a closed-end fund issues a fixed number of shares at the beginning to raise its capital in one go. This is what a company does in an initial public offering (IPO),* when it makes its shares available to the public for the first time; but in this case, the shares do not represent ownership in a company but participation in a "closed-end fund." Crucially, the price of these closed-end shares is not only a reflection of the assets the fund possesses and manages, but also a reflection of how many investors want to buy shares in it at the time.[2]

Sometimes the demand for shares in a closed-end fund is lower than that demanded by the market value of the fund's assets. In such cases, the price for the shares may be lower than it should be. This lower price represents an effective discount for those who do buy in at that price. If you buy shares in such a fund at such a discount and its assets match the overall performance of the market, you will in effect be gaining superior returns, since you bought in low.[3] That Malkiel still agrees with this analysis in the 2015 edition of *Random Walk* speaks to the solid ground of its conclusions.

It could be argued that all Malkiel's published works, even the influential "Valuation of Closed-End Investment Company Shares," are overshadowed by the huge achievement that is *A Random Walk*. As many of his other works provide additional commentary on and analysis of his random walk theory, his body of work can be considered highly coherent and unified.

Significance

While Malkiel was already a highly influential academic and successful investor, it is fair to say that *A Random Walk* is his best and most important work. Although the EMH was defined and demonstrated with empirical* data by the Nobel Prize-winning economist Eugene F. Fama,* Malkiel's books became the popular intellectual justification for long-term investment in broad-based index mutual funds, now a trillion-dollar business. The book's influence in investment theory and practice cannot be overestimated. He has been both praised and denounced by leading academic minds and famous billionaire investors such as the Americans George Soros* and Warren Buffett.*[4] The book has been cited thousands of times.

A Random Walk still defines Malkiel's reputation, despite his other published work. Some of the other subjects he has written about have a big presence in his theoretical and investing outlook, such as his focus on closed-end fund discounts, but in the public mind this is a small footnote to his random walk model. This theory asks the biggest of all questions when it comes to stocks: Can you predict what the market will do and so steadily earn superior returns on your investment? The entire financial industry has always said, and must always say, that you absolutely can if you're smart enough. Malkiel reached a popular audience with the message that beating the market is impossible. Because he has a huge body of sophisticated evidence to support this position, and was able to communicate it in accessible terms, Malkiel is the natural target for those experts and rival academics who want to attack the random walk theory and prove that stock prices *are* predictable.

Of particular significance was the makeup of the audience Malkiel reached with the text: the kind of "average investors" who are, he claims, constantly fleeced by Wall Street professionals claiming to possess insight that, in reality, cannot exist.

NOTES

1   Burton G. Malkiel, *A Random Walk Down Wall Street: The Time-Tested Strategy for Successful Investing* (New York: W.W. Norton & Company, 2015), 401.

2   Burton G. Malkiel, "The Valuation of Closed-End Investment Company Shares," Journal of Finance 32, no. 3 (June 1977): 847.

3   Malkiel, "The Valuation of Closed-End Investment Company Shares," 858.

4   For examples, see George Soros, "Soros: Financial Markets," *Financial Times*, October 17, 2009, accessed February 19, 2016, http://www.ft.com/intl/cms/s/2/dbc0e0c6-bfe9-11de-aed2-00144feab49a.html#axzz40d8gJlsO; and Warren Buffet, "The Superinvestors of Graham and Doddsville," *Hermes*, Columbia Business School Magazine, May 17, 1984.

SECTION 3
IMPACT

THE FIRST RESPONSES

KEY POINTS

- Although critics have claimed that price inefficiencies do exist in the stock* market and can be exploited for gain (that is, that it is possible to predict and exploit price fluctuations in the market), Malkiel says that in the long run, such inefficiencies disappear, so the efficient market hypothesis* (EMH) approach is still better.

- The world's most prominent investor, Warren Buffett,* maintains that there is much inefficiency in the market to be exploited; his successful investment record is compelling proof.

- Malkiel admits that price bubbles* have existed for centuries—but argues that although this is clearly irrational and inefficient market behavior, in the long term, bubbles burst and markets are efficient.

Criticism

The critical response to Burton G. Malkiel's *A Random Walk Down Wall Street: The Time-Tested Strategy for Successful Investing* has been mostly positive, particularly as research continues to show that stock markets are indeed efficient.[1] "Efficient" here means that the markets will find a price for each stock that accurately reflects all known information about the company it represents; if publically available information indicates that a company is doing well—or poorly—investors will bid the price of its stock up, or down. However, since the 1970s, the intellectual authority of the EMH has come under increasing attack as many financial economists and statisticians have come to believe that stock prices are at least partially predictable.[2]

> **❝ I'm convinced that there is much inefficiency in the market. ❞**
> Warren Buffett

One leading critical study by business researchers from the Massachusetts Institute of Technology (MIT) and the University of Pennsylvania was published with the (slightly mocking) title *A Non-Random Walk Down Wall Street* (1999). It challenged Malkiel's argument by showing mathematically that inefficiencies *do* exist in the stock market and can be exploited by active investors.[3] In the 11th edition of *A Random Walk*, Malkiel is happy to admit this point: "The stock market does not conform perfectly to the mathematician's ideal of the complete independence of present price movements from those of the past."[4] But his response is, so what? "The systematic relationships that exist are often so small that they are not useful to investors," he writes—they will be outweighed by the fees and capital gains tax* that come with frequent transactions.[5] In other words, it may sometimes happen that the stock price of a company that has performed strongly in the past will continue to rise more often than it will fall, simply due to investors' expectations. However, such "predictable" movements are likely to be small and if you give your money to investment professionals to try to take advantage of such distortions, the fees they charge will tend to wipe out any gains they can generate for you.

Other critics have argued that investors go through waves of excess optimism and pessimism, causing stock prices to deviate (go further up or down) in noticeable ways.[6] Other critics have detected "seasonal or day of the week" patterns; trading in January, for example, seems to take on certain regular features.[7] Indeed, Eugene F. Fama noticed in a 1993 study that over long periods of time, the stocks of smaller companies tend to generate larger returns than those of larger companies.[8]

Real-world investors have been the strongest critics, most notably the famous investor Warren Buffett,* who has publicly criticized the EMH. He claims that good investors search for "discrepancies between the *value* of a business and the *price* of small pieces of that business in the market"—that is, they use the approach known as fundamental analysis.*[9]

Responses

Malkiel has always answered challenges to his theory. In 2003, for example, he summarized his responses to all its major critics in an article "The Efficient Market Hypothesis and Its Critics." After listing his critics and explaining their arguments, he examines their investment strategies using empirical* evidence. He claims to show that "these patterns [of their supposedly successful investments] are not robust and dependable in different sample periods."[10] Moreover, he adds that "many of these patterns, even if they did exist, could self-destruct in the future, as many of them have already done."[11]

In other words, once word gets out about a market irregularity, it disappears. In a way this supports the EMH, since once a market advantage becomes widely known it quickly becomes the norm. Ultimately, Malkiel concludes that, "Our stock markets are far more efficient and far less predictable than some recent academic papers would have us believe"—a position he continues to hold.[12]

As for exceptional investors like Warren Buffett, who "beat the market" year after year, Malkiel takes a measured view. The 11th edition of *Random Walk* suggests that Warren Buffett's success is purely down to luck: "I have become increasingly convinced that the past records of mutual-fund managers are essentially worthless in predicting future success. The few examples of consistently superior performance occur no more frequently than can be expected by chance."[13] This is a very fair point: the random walk is bound to throw up a few long-term winners.

Conflict and Consensus

While the general opinion about the text is positive, the economists Charles P. Kindleberger* and Robert Z. Aliber* see the EMH as essentially resting on the rational belief that "investors react to changes in economic variables as if they are always fully aware of the long-term implications of each of these changes"—which is impossible.[14] This EMH assumption of "rational behavior" has been persuasively disputed by Kindleberger, Robert J. Shiller,* and others from the field of behavioral economics. Books like *A Non-Random Walk Down Wall Street* provide the empirical evidence to show that stock prices are predictable, and therefore that a bulletproof version of the EMH clearly does not hold.

But a perfectly reliable EMH is not what Malkiel ever really argues exists. *A Random Walk* clearly describes huge, irrational bubbles of the past—from the seventeenth-century Tulip Bulb Craze* in Holland to the subprime mortgage crisis* of the twenty-first century. Although this is not efficient market behavior, the fact that no one can always pinpoint when the market has reached its summit, and that even the cleverest investors sometimes get caught holding onto assets for too long (after their price has fallen considerably), proves the EMH in the longer term. As Malkiel puts it, "While the stock market in the short run may be a voting mechanism, in the long run it is a weighing mechanism. True value will win out in the end. Before the fact, there is no way in which investors can reliably exploit any anomalies or patterns that might exist."

Malkiel is careful to make claims for the EMH only in the long term—something his critics occasionally seem to overlook. Likewise, he maintains that the EMH would only be threatened by the long-term brilliance of a Warren Buffett if you could identify who these successful investors were going to be *before* their market-beating performance, rather than afterward.[15] "There will be some Warren Buffetts in the future," Malkiel admits. "There may be a few of them, but here is the problem: I don't know who they are and I don't think anyone else knows who they are; it's like looking for a needle in the haystack."[16]

NOTES

1 Jonathan Clarke, et al., "The Efficient Markets Hypothesis," in *Expert Financial Planning: Investment Strategies from Industry Leaders*, ed. Robert C. Arffa (New York: John Wiley & Sons, 2001), 132.

2 Burton G. Malkiel, "The Efficient Market Hypothesis and Its Critics," *Journal of Economic Perspectives,* 17 no. 1 (Winter, 2003): 60.

3 Andrew W. Lo and A. Craig MacKinlay, *A Non-Random Walk Down Wall Street* (Princeton; Oxford: Princeton University Press, 1999), 4.

4 Burton G. Malkiel, *A Random Walk Down Wall Street: The Time-Tested Strategy for Successful Investing* (New York: W.W. Norton & Company, 2015), 139.

5 *Random Walk,* 140.

6 Werner F. M. DeBondt and Richard Thaler, "Does the Stock Market Overreact?" *Journal of Finance* 40 (July, 1985): 793.

7 Robert A. Haugen and Josef Lakonishok, *The Incredible January Effect: The Stock Market's Unsolved Mystery* (Homewood: Dow Jones-Irwin,1987).

8 Malkiel, "The Efficient Market Hypothesis and Its Critics," 67–8.

9 Warren Buffett, "The Superinvestors of Graham and Doddsville," *The Columbia Business School Magazine* (May 17, 1984): 7.

10 Malkiel, "The Efficient Market Hypothesis and Its Critics," 71.

11 Malkiel, "The Efficient Market Hypothesis and Its Critics," 71.

12 Malkiel, "The Efficient Market Hypothesis and Its Critics," 60.

13 Malkiel, *Random Walk*, 398.

14 Robert Z. Aliber and Charles P. Kinderberger, *Manias, Panics, and Crashes: A History of Financial Crises* (London: Palgrave MacMillan, 2015), 53.

15 Clarke, "The Efficient Markets Hypothesis," 131.

16 Mac Greer, "Beating the Market is Like Believing in Santa Claus," *The Motley Fool*, accessed on November 25, 2014, http://www.fool.com/investing/general/2010/09/16/beating-the-market-is-like-believing-in-santa.aspx.

MODULE 10
THE EVOLVING DEBATE

KEY POINTS

- Although Malkiel's theory that the stock* market will always find the "right" price has become very popular, it is not easy to know if investors overreact or underreact to public news affecting a company's share prices (at least in the short term).

- New studies continue to show that simulations of monkeys throwing darts to pick shares could earn at least as much as many managed investment funds.

- Malkiel's popular intellectual justification for the efficient market hypothesis* (EMH) had a radical effect; although it remains controversial, *A Random Walk* is at the center of the ongoing debate about how the stock market works.

Uses and Problems

Burton G. Malkiel's *A Random Walk Down Wall Street: The Time-Tested Strategy for Successful Investing* was at the forefront of a new movement in investment theory and practice—one that said you could ignore the intelligence and expertise of individual investors and bet on the market itself. Critical to this is the careful definition of the EMH, which says that a stock's price captures all known information about its company at that moment.

To cite one rising challenge to the EMH: *how* investors generally react to public information can vary widely, and the "crowd" can overreact or underreact to relevant news. When they do, even when a stock price *is* purely driven by news, it is not always affected in the right way. These issues driving swings in market prices fall under the larger issue of irrational behavior in the market, which continues to

❝ The literature on the evidence for this [Random Walk] theory is well developed and includes work of the highest quality. Therefore, whether or not we ultimately agree with it, we must at least take the efficient market theory seriously. **❞**

Robert J. Shiller, *Irrational Exuberance*

challenge the EMH in important ways. For example, a sophisticated hedge fund* (a pool of money from different investors managed using high-risk methods) might buy into the rising bubble* of a stock price in order to "ride the momentum" upward and then (hopefully) get out in time. This flies in the face of Malkiel's claim that "smart rational traders will correct any mispricings that might arise from the presence of irrational traders."[1] In other words, according to Malkiel, smart investors will sell any stocks that seem to be rising in value as part of a price bubble, since that bubble could burst at any time, leaving them worse off. However, sometimes investors do the opposite for irrational reasons, like greed.

Schools of Thought

Over 40 years on, *A Random Walk* remains one of the most frequently cited investment books. There continue to be large numbers of securities* analysts, academics, and other investors who have either been influenced by it, or have been forced to confront it in promoting a different approach.

A Random Walk did not create a school of thought so much as reflect one: the rising tide of academics and investors who were beginning to question the performance of mutual fund managers, especially considering the high fees such managers typically charge. Citing the EMH, Malkiel's book famously claims that a blindfolded monkey throwing darts at a newspaper's financial pages can select stocks just as well as "experts."[2] The book can be seen as a challenge thrown at mutual fund* managers: "A monkey can do better than you."[3]

This monkey image has now taken on a life of its own. In 2014, the respected financial journal the *Economist* profiled several serious studies inspired by *A Random Walk*.[4] In separate experiments, two research groups, one in California and one at a London business school, tested the performance of fund managers against simulated monkeys throwing darts at the financial pages.[5] Their conclusions were that Malkiel was being too modest: "Simulating a dart-throwing monkey has resulted in portfolios* that would not just beat many investors, but also outperform the market."[6]

In Current Scholarship

These recent "monkey" studies reflect just how central Malkiel's book remains to discussions about how stock markets function, and demonstrate that the essential debate has not moved on that much. "Passive" index mutual funds* contain a broad portfolio of stocks to mirror the returns of the overall stock market. Over the long term, these continue to do well against more "actively" managed mutual funds—especially when the high manager fees, transaction fees, and capital gains tax* are factored in.

That said, a great deal of academic work continues to be done on the EMH, which includes asking the basic question as to how it compares to other investment strategies. Recent books *Principles of Corporate Finance* and *Financial Markets and Institutions* present the ongoing scholarly discussion about what exactly market efficiency* *is* (in terms of the EMH ideal).[7] Just how important the EMH is within today's world of investment and financial theory is another area of debate. Robert J. Shiller* won the 2013 Nobel Prize in Economics for his work on irrational behavior in markets, and ended up, uncomfortably, sharing the prize that year with Eugene F. Fama,* father of the EMH. Afterward, Shiller publicly repeated his opinion that the EMH is a "half-truth."[8]

Yet even recently, extensive data-based research continues to confirm the EMH when applied to the returns of individual companies and relevant indices[9] (that is, lists of companies). Nonetheless, the debate remains complicated: while the approach known as technical analysis* remains unpopular among academics (who see it as unprofitable), it is still widely applied by professionals. Some have suggested that the methods of technical analysis are not applied at their best when used in academic research.[10] Or it could be a delusion common to the world of investment, with money managers fooling themselves into believing it works, as Malkiel repeatedly argues in *A Random Walk*.

The economist Nassim Nicholas Taleb,* with his popular book *The Black Swan: The Impact of the Highly Improbable* (2007), could be seen as one of Malkiel's main successors. For Taleb, a successful financial manager in his own right, randomness is the determining factor not only in the stock market but also more generally. He claims that it is the highly improbable, highly impactful events that shape the world as we know it; but our reaction is to pretend that this randomness does not exist.[11] He goes on to explore the wider, psychological* human need to see the future as resembling the past. He points out that such understanding can provide a real financial edge, as it allows investors to protect themselves from the damage of destructive market events like the stock market crash of 2007–8.* Taleb sees the crash as "the result of fragility in systems built in ignorance" of the serious consequences of acting on uncertainty.[12]

NOTES

1   Burton G. Malkiel, *A Random Walk Down Wall Street: The Time-Tested Strategy for Successful Investing* (New York: W.W. Norton & Company, 2015), 230.

2   Malkiel, *Random Walk*, 26.

3   Malkiel, *Random Walk*, 19.

4   S. H., "No Monkey Business?" *Economist*, June 4, 2014, accessed on November 27, 2015, http://www.economist.com/blogs/freeexchange/2014/06/financial-knowledge-and-investment-performance.

5   Robert D. Arnott, et al., "The Surprising Alpha From Malkie's Monkey and Upside-Down Strategies," *The Journal of Portfolio Management*, 39, no. 4 (Summer, 2013); and Andrew Clare, et al., "An Evaluation of Alternative Equity Indices, Part 1," Cass Business School, City University London, March 2013, accessed on January 10, 2016, http://www.cassknowledge.com/sites/default/files/article-attachments/evaluation-alternative-equity-indices-part-1-cass-knowledge.pdf.

6   S. H., "No Monkey Business?"

7   F. Allen, et al., *Principles of Corporate Finance* (New York: McGraw-Hill/Irwin, 2011), 314– 320; G. Eakins and S. Mishkin, *Financial Markets and Institutions* (Boston: Prentice Hall, 2012), 117–130.

8   Robert J. Shiller, "Sharing Nobel Honors, and Agreeing to Disagree," *The New York Times*, accessed on 12 January, 2016, http://www.nytimes.com/2013/10/27/business/sharing-nobel-honors-and-agreeing-to-disagree.html?hp&_r=0.

9   R. W. Parks, and E. Zivot, "Financial market efficiency and its implications," *University of Washington, Investment, Capital and Finance*, accessed on 12 January, 2016, http://faculty.washington.edu/ezivot/econ422/Market%20Efficiency%20EZ.pdf.

10 Augustas Degutis and Lina Novickyte, "The Efficient Market Hypothesis: A Critical Review of Literature and Methodology," *Ekonomika* 93, no. 2 (2014): 12.

11 Nassim Nicholas Taleb, *The Black Swan: The Impact of the Highly Improbable* (London: Penguin, 2007), xxii.

12 Taleb, *The Black Swan*, 321.

IMPACT AND INFLUENCE TODAY

KEY POINTS

- Although investing has changed considerably, with the emergence of new theories and complex mathematical approaches in the decades since the first edition of *A Random Walk* was published in 1973, Malkiel claims that in long-term investments, finance professionals can still not perform better than "blindfolded monkeys."

- While the new models seek to exploit small stock* price inefficiencies to make profits, once fund managers' fees have been factored in the results are no better than those achieved by (passive) index funds.*

- Many academics and investors remain determined to prove that there *are* inefficiencies in the market to be consistently exploited by "experts," and therefore to disprove the efficient market hypothesis* (EMH).

Position

Over 40 years since its first publication, Burton G. Malkiel's *A Random Walk Down Wall Street: The Time-Tested Strategy for Successful Investing* remains a vital read for anyone interested in how the stock market works, or anyone looking to invest money in stocks. Its continued popularity suggests that, even while waves of skeptics continue to challenge its basic conclusion, Malkiel's book remains not only important but also persuasive.

These were decades that saw great economic change. The financial services industry* exploded in the United States, offering a new range of sophisticated strategies that all promised to "beat the market" (that is, to provide better earnings than the average increase in the value of

> ❝ A tremendous battle is going on, and it's fought with deadly intent because the stakes are tenure for the academics and bonuses for the professionals. That's why I think you'll enjoy this random walk down Wall Street. It has all the ingredients of high drama—including fortunes made and lost and classic arguments about their cause. ❞
>
> Burton G. Malkiel, *A Random Walk Down Wall Street*

stock market shares). These various approaches have had to address the efficient market hypothesis in general and Malkiel's book in particular. That a Wall Street fund manager could invest money better than a monkey was seen as a given before the first edition of *A Random Walk*. Since its publication, the abilities of investing professionals have been seriously challenged—threatening their generous earnings in the process.

The last four decades have also seen a revolution in statistical analysis,* and as a result, the ability to predict behavior through algorithms (a set of rules for solving mathematical problems) and other mathematical tools. Naturally these developments have been applied to making money via the stock market. As a result, quantitative analysts* (known as "quants") who try to predict market movements through mathematical equations, have become more important. Money managers use these new methods of analysis to try to prove that stock markets are predictable, and so pose a direct challenge to *A Random Walk* and the EMH.

Interaction

It is fair to say that many investment managers and academic theorists who take an "active" approach (believing they can beat the market by strategically buying and selling stocks) have a clear interest in disproving the EMH. An academic victory over the hypothesis would be valuable to Wall Street, restoring some public trust in the wisdom of mutual fund managers (suggesting that they are at least better than monkeys).

In the past few decades, a steady stream of new—often complicated—academic books have claimed that there are indeed exploitable inefficiencies in the market—such as very hard-to-see "trends" that can be used to predict price movements. In the 11th edition of *Random Walk*, Malkiel is happy to admit this point: "The stock market does not conform perfectly to the mathematician's ideal of the complete independence of present price movements from those of the past."[1] However, he maintains that "the systematic relationships that exist are often so small that they are not useful to investors."[2]

In the investment world, very few investors have used strategies that have beaten the market regularly over time. In the 11th edition of *Random Walk*, Malkiel claims that he harbors increasing doubts regarding even this select company: "In previous editions of this book, I provided the names of several investment managers who had enjoyed long-term records of successful portfolio management as well as brief biographies explaining their investment styles ... I have abandoned that practice in the current edition."[3] Malkiel has gradually grown ever more convinced that such success is simply due to chance.[4]

The Continuing Debate

Not only has the debate around Malkiel and the random walk theory failed to advance significantly over the past 40 years, Malkiel's responses to his challengers have not changed much either. Competition is so intense among fund managers, as each bids various stock prices closer to their true value, that it is almost impossible to outperform the market average over time. News gets factored into prices too quickly. Meanwhile, the generally good long-term performances of "passive" funds remain better than the performance of "active" funds, and cutting-edge equations have proven that small inefficiencies in the market are basically insignificant—they cannot produce higher earnings than the stock market average. The same goes for the advancing field of behavioral finance:* until these insights can translate into superior returns for investors over the long term, they cannot prove better than the EMH, in Malkiel's eyes.

That is not to say that behavioral finance is not impressive and developing fast—even Malkiel's latest edition of *A Random Walk* praises the insights and promise of the field—but in the end, the question is one of achieving higher returns over the long term. This practical focus on real investors is another reason for the enduring popularity of *A Random Walk*. As one commentator has put it, "Strictly speaking the EMH is false, but in spirit is profoundly true."[5] That is to say, in the short term there will always be bubbles,* wildly mispriced stocks and all sorts of irrational investor behavior, which would seem to disprove the EMH. In the long term however, empirical* data supports the position that bubbles will always burst, and prices will adjust to a (reasonably) accurate level. The long-term investor can depend on that to make money.

NOTES

1   Burton G. Malkiel, *A Random Walk Down Wall Street: The Time-Tested Strategy for Successful Investing,* (New York: W.W. Norton & Company, 2015), 139.

2   Malkiel, *Random Walk,* 140.

3   Malkiel, *Random Walk*, 398.

4   Malkiel, *Random Walk*, 398.

5   Martin Sewell, "History of the Efficient Market Hypothesis," *UCL Research Note* 11, no. 4 (January 20, 2011): 1.

MODULE 12
WHERE NEXT?

KEY POINTS

- While it is likely that *A Random Walk* will continue to be highly relevant, the financial crash of 2007–8* has thrown almost every economic belief into serious question and could also impact this book.

- *A Random Walk* will continue to affect conversations about price movements in the stock* market, even if the stock market itself is clearly entering a new, unpredictable era.

- The book is still one of the most cited and frequently mentioned texts in investment theory and practice, and has been for over 40 years; its influence, and the challenge it presents to "active" mutual fund managers, remains as strong as ever.

Potential

It seems likely that Burton G. Malkiel's *A Random Walk Down Wall Street: The Time-Tested Strategy for Successful Investing* will be a well-regarded and popular book about the stock market for years to come. Responses from top-notch investors and academics both to this work, and the efficient market hypothesis* (EMH) that it promotes, are bound to be ongoing. Many first-time investors will continue reading it in large numbers, absorbing its clear and accessible message.

That said, the state of most stock markets around the world (and the slowdown in the global economy generally) caused Malkiel to end his 11th edition with a cautionary note. He categorizes the post-Internet bubble* era of 2000 onwards as "The Age of Disenchantment," when "investors were again reminded that the world was a very risky place."[1] While there have been strong returns

> ❝ It would be unrealistic to anticipate that the generous returns earned by stock market investors during the 2009–2014 period can be expected during the years ahead. ❞
>
> Burton G. Malkiel, *A Random Walk Down Wall Street*

for investors over the past five years, particularly in the US stock market, this has largely been caused by a policy of "quantitative easing"* (the policy of printing cash and pumping it into the economy, raising the prices of most assets, especially stocks).

How such dramatic intervention by the federal government changes the basic dynamics of the stock market, and perhaps makes rising prices more predictable, is never addressed by Malkiel, which seems curious. He makes the prediction that "we are likely to be in a low-return environment for some time to come"[2] but does not speculate on how the earth-shaking effects of the US subprime mortgage crisis* might deeply change how the stock markets work. To imply that the stock market will function as it did from 1945–2008 may be a risky guess.

Future Directions

The core message of *A Random Walk* is that the world of investment is so competitive that no one has a long-term inside edge; so the movements of stock prices are totally unpredictable. This theory is likely to remain influential in the future even without the help of further research. New challenges from areas like behavioral finance* will continue to arise, but unless these rival schools of thought reveal a reliable way to "beat the market," they are unlikely to dislodge the importance of the EMH and Malkiel's popular text.

That said, *A Random Walk* does see price bubbles as short-term mistakes in pricings that get corrected in the longer term: the market itself pops them, and prices fall sharply. This may be true, but specialties like behavioral finance are needed to reveal just how such asset bubbles can get out of control, as happened during the US subprime mortgage crisis.* The then-chairman of the Federal Reserve* (America's central bank), Alan Greenspan,* took the view—both before and after the crash—that asset bubbles in the stock market and housing market need to be left alone to "pop" on their own.[3] In doing so he—like Malkiel and practically every other economist—had no idea about the huge financial structure that had been built on top of the housing bubble of the early 2000s. When it did finally pop, the flood of knock-on effects almost destroyed the entire economy.

A great deal of new theory and analysis is needed to ensure that this does not happen again. While the random walk theory* may be valid for understanding stock prices in normal conditions, it cannot protect the market against another disaster of this kind.

Summary

A Random Walk continues to educate the public about (or against) investment managers who claim to have privileged knowledge about the stock market. Malkiel's text discredits such promises in a convincing way by giving statistical examinations of popular "market-beating" strategies, undermining them further through the straightforward, gimmick-free logic of the EMH. For anyone planning to study investment or to invest in the stock market, *A Random Walk* remains essential reading.

Besides bringing together the major points of the EMH in a highly readable text, and attacking the idea that anyone can regularly "beat the market," Malkiel also shows a positive way forward for the investor. His recommendation that people buy and hold a broad-based index mutual fund* remains good advice—advice that people are taking. As he states in the 11th edition of *A Random Walk*, "During

2014, about one-third of the money invested by individuals and institutions was invested in index funds. And that percentage continues to grow."[4] Despite the system-wide crisis of the 2007–8 crash, Malkiel still firmly maintains that his time–tested strategy can meet an investor's needs in an uncertain future: "If you will follow the simple rules and timeless lessons espoused in this book, you are likely to do just fine, even during the toughest times."[5]

NOTES

1   Burton G. Malkiel, *A Random Walk Down Wall Street: The Time-Tested Strategy for Successful Investing* (New York: W.W. Norton & Company, 2015), 344.

2   Malkiel, *Random Walk*, 348.

3   For Greenspan's view both before and after the crash, see Alan Greenspan, "Greenspan's Bubble Bath," *Economist*, September 5, 2002, accessed February 19, 2016, http://www.economist.com/node/1314051; and "Alan Greenspan: The Fed Can't Prevent Market Bubbles," NewsMax Finance, July 24, 3014, accessed February 19, 2016, http://www.newsmax.com/Finance/StreetTalk/alan-greenspan-federal-reserve-bubbles-economy/2014/07/24/id/584744/.

4   Malkiel, *Random Walk*, 181.

5   Malkiel, *Random Walk*, 411.

GLOSSARY

GLOSSARY OF TERMS

American Finance Association: publisher of the *Journal of Finance,* the AFA is an organization founded on the scholarship of financial economics (knowledge of which it seeks to promote).

Behavioral finance: a field of finance studies exploring the psychological characteristics of people participating in the market, seeking to explain market movements and, in particular, repeated irrational errors.

Bubble: a conspicuous overpricing of assets.

Capital–asset pricing model: a model that claims that you must increase the total level of risk in a portfolio to earn superior returns.

Capital gains tax: tax on the increase in the value of shares (capital) that an investor must pay when selling those shares for more than was originally paid for them.

Closed–end fund: a fund that raises its capital only once by issuing a fixed number of shares; the price of these closed-end shares is not only a reflection of the assets the fund possesses and manages, but of how many investors want to buy shares in it at the time.

Dow Jones Industrial Average: a price-weighted average of 30 stocks traded on the New York stock exchange and the Nasdaq (the second-largest US stock exchange after New York), compiled to measure the performance of the industrial sector of the American economy.

Economics: the social science describing the production, distribution, and consumption of scarce resources in a world of unlimited wants.

Efficiency: in the discipline of economics, this is a state where all resources are optimally allocated. In the stock exchange, it means a stock price that comes closest to the true value of the company in which it represents ownership.

Efficient market hypothesis (EMH): the idea that asset prices, including stock prices, capture all available information about that asset or respective company.

Empirical: relating to information verifiable by observation, and the conclusions based on that information, rather than on theory.

Federal Reserve: the central bank of the United States that regulates the nation's monetary and financial systems.

Financial crash of 2007–8: an event that triggered the biggest worldwide decline since the Great Depression of the 1930s. It was caused by the rapid growth in overpriced securities tied to a very risky housing market (especially in the United States). The crash saw many billions of dollars lost on stock markets around the world.

Financial services industry: the economic services provided by a broad range of businesses in a given country. These include banks, insurance companies, credit unions, real estate companies, and so forth.

Fundamental analysis: a method of evaluating a security, such as a bond or stock share, by measuring its "intrinsic value"—what it is really worth in the market as opposed to how it is currently priced.

Global economic recession of 2007–9: the biggest worldwide decline since the Great Depression of the 1930s. It was triggered by the rapid growth in securities tied to the subprime (highly risky) housing market, especially in the United States. When this collapsed, it caused the bankruptcy of major financial institutions around the world, and government bail-outs to prevent greater chaos.

Great Depression: a catastrophic economic downturn that began in the United States in the 1920s, soon spreading to Europe, notably Great Britain, and continuing into the 1930s.

Hedge fund: a pool of money collected from a group of investors and then managed by a general partner, who aims to maximize investor returns whether the market climbs or declines. Hedge funds often use high-risk methods, such as investing with borrowed money.

Index fund/index mutual fund: a portfolio of diverse stocks, intentionally selected to provide broad market exposure and allow the performance of a portfolio to mirror that of the overall stock market.

Insider information: non-public information about the state of a publicly traded company. Such information typically gives an advantage to buyers and sellers of that company's stock. Using insider information in this way is illegal.

Initial public offering (IPO): the first time a privately owned company issues shares and sells them to the public. The company will also call this moment "going public."

Modern portfolio theory: an attempt to maximize the return (earnings) of a portfolio of stocks, bonds, or other assets. It attempts to minimize the risks by choosing various assets whose risks offset each other.

Mutual fund: a pool of money collected from a group of investors used to purchase various securities such as stocks and bonds, the profits of which the investors share in proportion to the amount of money each has contributed.

New York stock exchange: a market where various companies are publicly listed in order to ease trading with investors. It is located in New York City and is the largest stock exchange in the world.

Ponzi scheme: a fraud whereby high rates of return are promised to investors, with little risk. The returns are paid to investors from the money provided by new investors. As long as more new investors enter the scheme, earlier investors receive their promised returns. All but the early investors tend to lose their money.

Psychology: the study of the human mind and behavior.

Quantitative analysis: the evaluation of financial markets through often-complex mathematical and statistical modeling. This method seeks to turn mass amounts of information about a market into insight about how it will perform in the future.

Quantitative easing: the policy of printing cash and pumping it into the economy, raising the prices of most assets, especially stocks.

Random walk theory: a financial theory that states prices cannot be predicted, because future price movements bear no relation to past price movements. Such an idea is closely related to the efficient market hypothesis.

Randomness: a complete lack of predictability of events or sequences.

Security: a financial agreement showing ownership in a publicly traded corporation (stock) or a promise of repayment for a loan to a governmental body or a corporation (bond).

"Smart beta" strategies: investment schemes that create an index of purchased stocks, seeking to take advantage of perceived systematic biases or inefficiencies in the market.

Speculator: for Malkiel, a speculator is someone who buys stocks hoping for a short-term gain.

Stocks: securities that provide a share of ownership in a corporation and therefore a claim on its future assets and earnings.

Subprime real estate market: the lower end of the housing market, involving those who are least able to afford to pay their mortgages. Investment in the subprime real estate market is therefore particularly risky.

Systemic risk: refers to the risk that an entire financial market or entire financial system will collapse, rather than the risk entailed by investing in one aspect of the overall system, such as a company. Investing in a company always exposes you to both forms of risk.

Technical analysis: a strategy for predicting the future price of securities through the evaluation of past prices and volume, among other statistics.

Tulip Bulb Craze: a period in seventeenth-century Holland when the contract prices for bulbs of the newly distributed (but still relatively rare) tulips reached astronomical prices, and then collapsed.

Vanguard Group: a US investment management company that is the largest provider of (primarily index) mutual funds and the second-largest provider or exchange-traded funds in the world as of March 2015. It manages over $3 trillion in assets.

US subprime mortgage crisis: A 2007–08 financial crisis in the United Stated that spread globally. It was triggered by a huge fall in real estate prices, leading to foreclosures, mortgage delinquencies (especially among poorer, "subprime" markets) and eventually sudden insolvencies among large banks and financial firms. Household spending also fell sharply as the world entered a global economic recession.

World War II (1939–45): a global conflict fought between the Axis powers (Germany, Italy, and Japan) and the victorious Allied powers (United Kingdom and its colonies, the former Soviet Union, the United States, and others).

PEOPLE MENTIONED IN THE TEXT

Louis Bechelier (1870–1946) was a French mathematician. He is often credited with having written the first paper that applied advanced mathematics to the study of finance.

John Bogle (b. 1929) is an economist and investor from the United States. He is the founder and retired CEO of The Vanguard Group and creator of the first index mutual fund. His book *Common Sense on Mutual Funds* (1999) was a best seller and is considered a classic within the investment community.

Warren Buffett (b. 1930) is a famous investor. He is the chairman and CEO of the investment fund Berkshire Hathaway, and one of the world's wealthiest people. He credits his successful investment to fundamental analysis, and has publicly questioned the efficient market hypothesis.

Andrea Coombes (b. 1965) is an award-winning American journalist, personal finance columnist and editor. She sees *A Random Walk Down Wall Street* as one of the most important books for new investors.

Charles D. Ellis (b. 1937) is an American investment consultant, and believer in index mutual funds. In 1975 he wrote "The Loser's Game" which publicly questioned the performance of nearly every mutual fund manager.

Eugene F. Fama (b. 1939) is a Nobel Prize-winning economist from the United States whose focus has been the analysis of stock market behavior. He is credited with making the efficient market hypothesis credible through empirical evidence.

Milton Friedman (1912–2006) was an American Nobel Prize-winning economist specializing in monetary policy. His theories were particularly influential in the 1980s, and continue to influence conservative economic policy today.

Alan Greenspan (b. 1926) was the chairman of the Federal Reserve, the US central bank, from 1987 to 2006.

Michael Jensen (b. 1939) is an American economist and emeritus professor at Harvard University, who specializes in the field of finance.

John Maynard Keynes (1883–1946) was an English economist whose macroeconomic theories radically changed the field, and formed the basis for today's "Keynesian school" of economics. He was a believer in technical analysis—that past trends in stock prices could help predict future ones.

Peter Lynch (b. 1944) is an investor who managed the Magellan Fund from 1977–1990, achieving a 29.2 percent average annual rate of return. He consistently "beat the market."

Paul A. Samuelson (1915–2009) was the first American to win the Nobel Memorial Prize in Economic Sciences and has been called the "father of modern economics." In the 1970s he publicly questioned the performance of mutual fund managers.

Fred Schwed was an American stockbroker. He was the author of *Where Are the Customers' Yachts?* (1940), which publicly mocked the value of Wall Street professionals.

Robert J. Shiller (b. 1946) is a Nobel Prize-winning economist and author of *Irrational Exuberance* (2000). His work in financial economics and behavioral finance is skeptical of the efficient market hypothesis.

George Soros (b. 1930) is one of the world's wealthiest and most famous investors. He is chairman of Soros Fund Management and an open skeptic of the efficient market hypothesis.

Nassim Nicholas Taleb (b. 1960) is a Lebanese American author and investor. His work on the nature of randomness and uncertainty has had an impact on the worlds of finance and philosophy, among other disciplines.

WORKS CITED

WORKS CITED

Aliber, Robert Z., and Charles P. Kindleberger. *Manias, Panics, and Crashes: A History of Financial Crises*. Palgrave MacMillan: London, 2015.

Allen, Franklin, Richard Brealey, and Stewart Myers. *Principles of Corporate Finance*. McGraw-Hill/Irwin: New York, 2011.

Arnott, Robert D., Jason Hsu, Vitali Kalesnik, and Phil Tindall. "The Surprising Alpha From Malkiel's Monkey and Upside-Down Strategies." *Journal of Portfolio Management* 39, no. 4 (summer 2013): 91–105.

Buffett, Warren. "2014 Letter to Shareholders." Accessed February 15, 2016. http://www.berkshirehathaway.com/letters/2013ltr.pdf.

————. "The Superinvestors of Graham and Doddsville." *Hermes,* Columbia Business School Magazine (May 17, 1984).

Clare, Andrew, Nick Motson, and Steve Thomas. "An Evaluation of Alternative Equity Indices. Part 1: Heuristic and Optimised Weighting Schemes." Cass Business School, City University London, March 2013. Accessed February 15, 2016. http://www.cassknowledge.com/sites/default/files/article-attachments/evaluation-alternative-equity-indices-part-1-cass-knowledge.pdf.

Clarke, Jonathan, Tomas Jandik, and Gershon Mandelker. "The Efficient Markets Hypothesis." In *Expert Financial Planning: Investment Strategies from Industry Leaders,* edited by Robert C. Arffa. New York: John Wiley & Sons, 2001.

Coombes, Andrea. "Financial Literacy 101: Where to Begin." *The Wall Street Journal*. Accessed February 15, 2016. http://www.wsj.com/articles/SB100014241278873245563045781174041313 72338.

DeBondt, Werner F. M., and Richard Thaler. "Does the Stock Market Overreact?" *Journal of Finance* 40, no. 3 (July 1985): 793–805.

Degutis, Augustas, and Lina Novickyte, "The Efficient Market Hypothesis: A Critical Review of Literature and Methodology." *Ekonomika* 93, no. 2 (2014).

Dunn, Douglas H. *Ponzi*. New York: McGraw-Hill, 1975.

Eakins, G., and S. Mishkin. *Financial Markets and Institutions.* Boston: Prentice Hall, 2012.

Ellis, Charles D. "The Loser's Game." *Financial Analysts Journal* 31, no. 4 (July/August 1975): 19–26.

Fama, Eugene F. "Efficient Markets: A Review of Theory and Empirical Work." *Journal of Finance* 25, no. 2 (May, 1970): 383–417.

Friedman, Milton and Anna Jacobson Schwartz. *A Monetary History of the United States, 1867–1960*. Princeton: Princeton University Press, 1963.

Greenspan, Alan. "Alan Greenspan: The Fed Can't Prevent Market Bubbles." NewsMax Finance, July 24, 3014. Accessed February 19, 2016. http://www.newsmax.com/Finance/StreetTalk/alan-greenspan-federal-reserve-bubbles-economy/2014/07/24/id/584744/.

— — —. "Greenspan's Bubble Bath." *Economist*, September 5, 2002. Accessed February 19, 2016. http://www.economist.com/node/1314051.

Greer, Mac. "Beating the Market is Like Believing in Santa Claus." *The Motley Fool,* September 16, 2010. Accessed February 16, 2016.

http://www.fool.com/investing/general/2010/09/16/beating-the-market-is-like-believing-in-santa.aspx.

H. S. "No Monkey Business?" *Economist*, June 4, 2014. Accessed February 16, 2016. http://www.economist.com/blogs/freeexchange/2014/06/financial-knowledge-and-investment-performance.

Keynes, John Maynard. *The General Theory of Employment, Interest and Money.* London: Macmillan, 1936.

Krugman, Paul and Robin Wells. "The Busts Keep Getting Bigger: Why?" *New York Review of Books*, July 14, 2011.

Lo, Andrew W., and A. Craig MacKinlay. *A Non-Random Walk Down Wall Street*. Princeton; Oxford: Princeton University Press, 1999.

Majouji, Ramy. "The Financial Markets Context." Open University OpenLearn. Accessed February 16, 2016. http://www.open.edu/openlearn/money-management/money/accounting-and-finance/the-financial-markets-context/content-section—acknowledgements.

Malkiel, Burton G. "The Efficient Market Hypothesis and Its Critics." *Journal of Economic Perspectives* 17, no. 1 (Winter, 2003).

— — —. *A Random Walk Down Wall Street: The Time-Tested Strategy for Successful Investing.* New York: W.W. Norton & Company, 2015.

— — —. "The Valuation of Closed-End Investment Company Shares." *Journal of Finance* 32, no. 3 (June 1977): 847–59.

The Motley Fool. "Investment Greats: Burton Malkiel." Accessed February 16, 2016. http://news.fool.co.uk/news/investing/2011/01/04/investment-greats-burton-malkiel.aspx.

Parks, R. W. and Zivot, E. "Financial Market Efficiency and Its Implications." University of Washington Investment, Capital and Finance, 2006. Accessed February 16, 2016. http://faculty.washington.edu/ezivot/econ422/Market%20 Efficiency%20EZ.pdf.

Ro, Sam. "Finance Wizard Burton Malkiel Defends the Efficient Market Hypothesis." *Business Insider UK.* Accessed February 16, 2016. http://www.businessinsider.com/burton-malkiel-efficient-market-hypothesis-2012-4?IR=T.

Samuelson, Paul A. "Challenge to Judgment." *Journal of Portfolio Management* 1, no. 1 (Fall 1974).

Schwed, Fred Jr. *Where Are the Customers' Yachts?* Hoboken, NJ: John Wiley & Sons, 2006.

Sewell, Martin. "History of the Efficient Market Hypothesis." *University College London Research Note* 11, no. 4 (January 20, 2011).

Shiller, Robert J. *Irrational Exuberance.* Princeton: Princeton University Press, 2000.

———. "Sharing Nobel Honors, and Agreeing to Disagree." *New York Times*, October 26, 2013. Accessed February 16, 2016. http://www.nytimes.com/2013/10/27/business/sharing-nobel-honors-and-agreeing-to-disagree.html?hp&_r=0.

Soros, George. "Soros: Financial Markets." *Financial Times*, October 27, 2009. Accessed February 19, 2016. http://www.ft.com/intl/cms/s/2/dbc0e0c6-bfe9-11de-aed2-00144feab49a.html#axzz40d8gJIsO

Taleb, Nassim Nicholas. *The Black Swan: The Impact of the Highly Improbable.* London: Penguin: 2007.

Udland, Myles. "30 Years Ago Warren Buffett Gave Away The Secret To Good Investing And Correctly Predicted No One Would Listen." *Business Insider UK*, August 14, 2014. Accessed February 16, 2015. http://uk.businessinsider.com/warren-buffett-graham-and-doddsville-lecture-2014-8?r=US&IR=T.

Wealthfront company website. Accessed February 16, 2016. https://www.wealthfront.com/our-beliefs.

THE MACAT LIBRARY
BY DISCIPLINE

AFRICANA STUDIES

Chinua Achebe's *An Image of Africa: Racism in Conrad's Heart of Darkness*
W. E. B. Du Bois's *The Souls of Black Folk*
Zora Neale Huston's *Characteristics of Negro Expression*
Martin Luther King Jr's *Why We Can't Wait*
Toni Morrison's *Playing in the Dark: Whiteness in the American Literary Imagination*

ANTHROPOLOGY

Arjun Appadurai's *Modernity at Large: Cultural Dimensions of Globalisation*
Philippe Ariès's *Centuries of Childhood*
Franz Boas's *Race, Language and Culture*
Kim Chan & Renée Mauborgne's *Blue Ocean Strategy*
Jared Diamond's *Guns, Germs & Steel: the Fate of Human Societies*
Jared Diamond's *Collapse: How Societies Choose to Fail or Survive*
E. E. Evans-Pritchard's *Witchcraft, Oracles and Magic Among the Azande*
James Ferguson's *The Anti-Politics Machine*
Clifford Geertz's *The Interpretation of Cultures*
David Graeber's *Debt: the First 5000 Years*
Karen Ho's *Liquidated: An Ethnography of Wall Street*
Geert Hofstede's *Culture's Consequences: Comparing Values, Behaviors, Institutes and Organizations across Nations*
Claude Lévi-Strauss's *Structural Anthropology*
Jay Macleod's *Ain't No Makin' It: Aspirations and Attainment in a Low-Income Neighborhood*
Saba Mahmood's *The Politics of Piety: The Islamic Revival and the Feminist Subject*
Marcel Mauss's *The Gift*

BUSINESS

Jean Lave & Etienne Wenger's *Situated Learning*
Theodore Levitt's *Marketing Myopia*
Burton G. Malkiel's *A Random Walk Down Wall Street*
Douglas McGregor's *The Human Side of Enterprise*
Michael Porter's *Competitive Strategy: Creating and Sustaining Superior Performance*
John Kotter's *Leading Change*
C. K. Prahalad & Gary Hamel's *The Core Competence of the Corporation*

CRIMINOLOGY

Michelle Alexander's *The New Jim Crow: Mass Incarceration in the Age of Colorblindness*
Michael R. Gottfredson & Travis Hirschi's *A General Theory of Crime*
Richard Herrnstein & Charles A. Murray's *The Bell Curve: Intelligence and Class Structure in American Life*
Elizabeth Loftus's *Eyewitness Testimony*
Jay Macleod's *Ain't No Makin' It: Aspirations and Attainment in a Low-Income Neighborhood*
Philip Zimbardo's *The Lucifer Effect*

ECONOMICS

Janet Abu-Lughod's *Before European Hegemony*
Ha-Joon Chang's *Kicking Away the Ladder*
David Brion Davis's *The Problem of Slavery in the Age of Revolution*
Milton Friedman's *The Role of Monetary Policy*
Milton Friedman's *Capitalism and Freedom*
David Graeber's *Debt: the First 5000 Years*
Friedrich Hayek's *The Road to Serfdom*
Karen Ho's *Liquidated: An Ethnography of Wall Street*

John Maynard Keynes's *The General Theory of Employment, Interest and Money*
Charles P. Kindleberger's *Manias, Panics and Crashes*
Robert Lucas's *Why Doesn't Capital Flow from Rich to Poor Countries?*
Burton G. Malkiel's *A Random Walk Down Wall Street*
Thomas Robert Malthus's *An Essay on the Principle of Population*
Karl Marx's *Capital*
Thomas Piketty's *Capital in the Twenty-First Century*
Amartya Sen's *Development as Freedom*
Adam Smith's *The Wealth of Nations*
Nassim Nicholas Taleb's *The Black Swan: The Impact of the Highly Improbable*
Amos Tversky's & Daniel Kahneman's *Judgment under Uncertainty: Heuristics and Biases*
Mahbub Ul Haq's *Reflections on Human Development*
Max Weber's *The Protestant Ethic and the Spirit of Capitalism*

FEMINISM AND GENDER STUDIES

Judith Butler's *Gender Trouble*
Simone De Beauvoir's *The Second Sex*
Michel Foucault's *History of Sexuality*
Betty Friedan's *The Feminine Mystique*
Saba Mahmood's *The Politics of Piety: The Islamic Revival and the Feminist Subject*
Joan Wallach Scott's *Gender and the Politics of History*
Mary Wollstonecraft's *A Vindication of the Rights of Woman*
Virginia Woolf's *A Room of One's Own*

GEOGRAPHY

The Brundtland Report's *Our Common Future*
Rachel Carson's *Silent Spring*
Charles Darwin's *On the Origin of Species*
James Ferguson's *The Anti-Politics Machine*
Jane Jacobs's *The Death and Life of Great American Cities*
James Lovelock's *Gaia: A New Look at Life on Earth*
Amartya Sen's *Development as Freedom*
Mathis Wackernagel & William Rees's *Our Ecological Footprint*

HISTORY

Janet Abu-Lughod's *Before European Hegemony*
Benedict Anderson's *Imagined Communities*
Bernard Bailyn's *The Ideological Origins of the American Revolution*
Hanna Batatu's *The Old Social Classes And The Revolutionary Movements Of Iraq*
Christopher Browning's *Ordinary Men: Reserve Police Batallion 101 and the Final Solution in Poland*
Edmund Burke's *Reflections on the Revolution in France*
William Cronon's *Nature's Metropolis: Chicago And The Great West*
Alfred W. Crosby's *The Columbian Exchange*
Hamid Dabashi's *Iran: A People Interrupted*
David Brion Davis's *The Problem of Slavery in the Age of Revolution*
Nathalie Zemon Davis's *The Return of Martin Guerre*
Jared Diamond's *Guns, Germs & Steel: the Fate of Human Societies*
Frank Dikotter's *Mao's Great Famine*
John W Dower's *War Without Mercy: Race And Power In The Pacific War*
W. E. B. Du Bois's *The Souls of Black Folk*
Richard J. Evans's *In Defence of History*
Lucien Febvre's *The Problem of Unbelief in the 16th Century*
Sheila Fitzpatrick's *Everyday Stalinism*

The Macat Library By Discipline

Eric Foner's *Reconstruction: America's Unfinished Revolution, 1863-1877*
Michel Foucault's *Discipline and Punish*
Michel Foucault's *History of Sexuality*
Francis Fukuyama's *The End of History and the Last Man*
John Lewis Gaddis's *We Now Know: Rethinking Cold War History*
Ernest Gellner's *Nations and Nationalism*
Eugene Genovese's *Roll, Jordan, Roll: The World the Slaves Made*
Carlo Ginzburg's *The Night Battles*
Daniel Goldhagen's *Hitler's Willing Executioners*
Jack Goldstone's *Revolution and Rebellion in the Early Modern World*
Antonio Gramsci's *The Prison Notebooks*
Alexander Hamilton, John Jay & James Madison's *The Federalist Papers*
Christopher Hill's *The World Turned Upside Down*
Carole Hillenbrand's *The Crusades: Islamic Perspectives*
Thomas Hobbes's *Leviathan*
Eric Hobsbawm's *The Age Of Revolution*
John A. Hobson's *Imperialism: A Study*
Albert Hourani's *History of the Arab Peoples*
Samuel P. Huntington's *The Clash of Civilizations and the Remaking of World Order*
C. L. R. James's *The Black Jacobins*
Tony Judt's *Postwar: A History of Europe Since 1945*
Ernst Kantorowicz's *The King's Two Bodies: A Study in Medieval Political Theology*
Paul Kennedy's *The Rise and Fall of the Great Powers*
Ian Kershaw's *The "Hitler Myth": Image and Reality in the Third Reich*
John Maynard Keynes's *The General Theory of Employment, Interest and Money*
Charles P. Kindleberger's *Manias, Panics and Crashes*
Martin Luther King Jr's *Why We Can't Wait*
Henry Kissinger's *World Order: Reflections on the Character of Nations and the Course of History*
Thomas Kuhn's *The Structure of Scientific Revolutions*
Georges Lefebvre's *The Coming of the French Revolution*
John Locke's *Two Treatises of Government*
Niccolò Machiavelli's *The Prince*
Thomas Robert Malthus's *An Essay on the Principle of Population*
Mahmood Mamdani's *Citizen and Subject: Contemporary Africa And The Legacy Of Late Colonialism*
Karl Marx's *Capital*
Stanley Milgram's *Obedience to Authority*
John Stuart Mill's *On Liberty*
Thomas Paine's *Common Sense*
Thomas Paine's *Rights of Man*
Geoffrey Parker's *Global Crisis: War, Climate Change and Catastrophe in the Seventeenth Century*
Jonathan Riley-Smith's *The First Crusade and the Idea of Crusading*
Jean-Jacques Rousseau's *The Social Contract*
Joan Wallach Scott's *Gender and the Politics of History*
Theda Skocpol's *States and Social Revolutions*
Adam Smith's *The Wealth of Nations*
Timothy Snyder's *Bloodlands: Europe Between Hitler and Stalin*
Sun Tzu's *The Art of War*
Keith Thomas's *Religion and the Decline of Magic*
Thucydides's *The History of the Peloponnesian War*
Frederick Jackson Turner's *The Significance of the Frontier in American History*
Odd Arne Westad's *The Global Cold War: Third World Interventions And The Making Of Our Times*

LITERATURE

Chinua Achebe's *An Image of Africa: Racism in Conrad's Heart of Darkness*
Roland Barthes's *Mythologies*
Homi K. Bhabha's *The Location of Culture*
Judith Butler's *Gender Trouble*
Simone De Beauvoir's *The Second Sex*
Ferdinand De Saussure's *Course in General Linguistics*
T. S. Eliot's *The Sacred Wood: Essays on Poetry and Criticism*
Zora Neale Huston's *Characteristics of Negro Expression*
Toni Morrison's *Playing in the Dark: Whiteness in the American Literary Imagination*
Edward Said's *Orientalism*
Gayatri Chakravorty Spivak's *Can the Subaltern Speak?*
Mary Wollstonecraft's *A Vindication of the Rights of Women*
Virginia Woolf's *A Room of One's Own*

PHILOSOPHY

Elizabeth Anscombe's *Modern Moral Philosophy*
Hannah Arendt's *The Human Condition*
Aristotle's *Metaphysics*
Aristotle's *Nicomachean Ethics*
Edmund Gettier's *Is Justified True Belief Knowledge?*
Georg Wilhelm Friedrich Hegel's *Phenomenology of Spirit*
David Hume's *Dialogues Concerning Natural Religion*
David Hume's *The Enquiry for Human Understanding*
Immanuel Kant's *Religion within the Boundaries of Mere Reason*
Immanuel Kant's *Critique of Pure Reason*
Søren Kierkegaard's *The Sickness Unto Death*
Søren Kierkegaard's *Fear and Trembling*
C. S. Lewis's *The Abolition of Man*
Alasdair MacIntyre's *After Virtue*
Marcus Aurelius's *Meditations*
Friedrich Nietzsche's *On the Genealogy of Morality*
Friedrich Nietzsche's *Beyond Good and Evil*
Plato's *Republic*
Plato's *Symposium*
Jean-Jacques Rousseau's *The Social Contract*
Gilbert Ryle's *The Concept of Mind*
Baruch Spinoza's *Ethics*
Sun Tzu's *The Art of War*
Ludwig Wittgenstein's *Philosophical Investigations*

POLITICS

Benedict Anderson's *Imagined Communities*
Aristotle's *Politics*
Bernard Bailyn's *The Ideological Origins of the American Revolution*
Edmund Burke's *Reflections on the Revolution in France*
John C. Calhoun's *A Disquisition on Government*
Ha-Joon Chang's *Kicking Away the Ladder*
Hamid Dabashi's *Iran: A People Interrupted*
Hamid Dabashi's *Theology of Discontent: The Ideological Foundation of the Islamic Revolution in Iran*
Robert Dahl's *Democracy and its Critics*
Robert Dahl's *Who Governs?*
David Brion Davis's *The Problem of Slavery in the Age of Revolution*

The Macat Library By Discipline

Alexis De Tocqueville's *Democracy in America*
James Ferguson's *The Anti-Politics Machine*
Frank Dikotter's *Mao's Great Famine*
Sheila Fitzpatrick's *Everyday Stalinism*
Eric Foner's *Reconstruction: America's Unfinished Revolution, 1863-1877*
Milton Friedman's *Capitalism and Freedom*
Francis Fukuyama's *The End of History and the Last Man*
John Lewis Gaddis's *We Now Know: Rethinking Cold War History*
Ernest Gellner's *Nations and Nationalism*
David Graeber's *Debt: the First 5000 Years*
Antonio Gramsci's *The Prison Notebooks*
Alexander Hamilton, John Jay & James Madison's *The Federalist Papers*
Friedrich Hayek's *The Road to Serfdom*
Christopher Hill's *The World Turned Upside Down*
Thomas Hobbes's *Leviathan*
John A. Hobson's *Imperialism: A Study*
Samuel P. Huntington's *The Clash of Civilizations and the Remaking of World Order*
Tony Judt's *Postwar: A History of Europe Since 1945*
David C. Kang's *China Rising: Peace, Power and Order in East Asia*
Paul Kennedy's *The Rise and Fall of Great Powers*
Robert Keohane's *After Hegemony*
Martin Luther King Jr.'s *Why We Can't Wait*
Henry Kissinger's *World Order: Reflections on the Character of Nations and the Course of History*
John Locke's *Two Treatises of Government*
Niccolò Machiavelli's *The Prince*
Thomas Robert Malthus's *An Essay on the Principle of Population*
Mahmood Mamdani's *Citizen and Subject: Contemporary Africa And The Legacy Of Late Colonialism*
Karl Marx's *Capital*
John Stuart Mill's *On Liberty*
John Stuart Mill's *Utilitarianism*
Hans Morgenthau's *Politics Among Nations*
Thomas Paine's *Common Sense*
Thomas Paine's *Rights of Man*
Thomas Piketty's *Capital in the Twenty-First Century*
Robert D. Putman's *Bowling Alone*
John Rawls's *Theory of Justice*
Jean-Jacques Rousseau's *The Social Contract*
Theda Skocpol's *States and Social Revolutions*
Adam Smith's *The Wealth of Nations*
Sun Tzu's *The Art of War*
Henry David Thoreau's *Civil Disobedience*
Thucydides's *The History of the Peloponnesian War*
Kenneth Waltz's *Theory of International Politics*
Max Weber's *Politics as a Vocation*
Odd Arne Westad's *The Global Cold War: Third World Interventions And The Making Of Our Times*

POSTCOLONIAL STUDIES

Roland Barthes's *Mythologies*
Frantz Fanon's *Black Skin, White Masks*
Homi K. Bhabha's *The Location of Culture*
Gustavo Gutiérrez's *A Theology of Liberation*
Edward Said's *Orientalism*
Gayatri Chakravorty Spivak's *Can the Subaltern Speak?*

PSYCHOLOGY

Gordon Allport's *The Nature of Prejudice*
Alan Baddeley & Graham Hitch's *Aggression: A Social Learning Analysis*
Albert Bandura's *Aggression: A Social Learning Analysis*
Leon Festinger's *A Theory of Cognitive Dissonance*
Sigmund Freud's *The Interpretation of Dreams*
Betty Friedan's *The Feminine Mystique*
Michael R. Gottfredson & Travis Hirschi's *A General Theory of Crime*
Eric Hoffer's *The True Believer: Thoughts on the Nature of Mass Movements*
William James's *Principles of Psychology*
Elizabeth Loftus's *Eyewitness Testimony*
A. H. Maslow's *A Theory of Human Motivation*
Stanley Milgram's *Obedience to Authority*
Steven Pinker's *The Better Angels of Our Nature*
Oliver Sacks's *The Man Who Mistook His Wife For a Hat*
Richard Thaler & Cass Sunstein's *Nudge: Improving Decisions About Health, Wealth and Happiness*
Amos Tversky's *Judgment under Uncertainty: Heuristics and Biases*
Philip Zimbardo's *The Lucifer Effect*

SCIENCE

Rachel Carson's *Silent Spring*
William Cronon's *Nature's Metropolis: Chicago And The Great West*
Alfred W. Crosby's *The Columbian Exchange*
Charles Darwin's *On the Origin of Species*
Richard Dawkin's *The Selfish Gene*
Thomas Kuhn's *The Structure of Scientific Revolutions*
Geoffrey Parker's *Global Crisis: War, Climate Change and Catastrophe in the Seventeenth Century*
Mathis Wackernagel & William Rees's *Our Ecological Footprint*

SOCIOLOGY

Michelle Alexander's *The New Jim Crow: Mass Incarceration in the Age of Colorblindness*
Gordon Allport's *The Nature of Prejudice*
Albert Bandura's *Aggression: A Social Learning Analysis*
Hanna Batatu's *The Old Social Classes And The Revolutionary Movements Of Iraq*
Ha-Joon Chang's *Kicking Away the Ladder*
W. E. B. Du Bois's *The Souls of Black Folk*
Émile Durkheim's *On Suicide*
Frantz Fanon's *Black Skin, White Masks*
Frantz Fanon's *The Wretched of the Earth*
Eric Foner's *Reconstruction: America's Unfinished Revolution, 1863-1877*
Eugene Genovese's *Roll, Jordan, Roll: The World the Slaves Made*
Jack Goldstone's *Revolution and Rebellion in the Early Modern World*
Antonio Gramsci's *The Prison Notebooks*
Richard Herrnstein & Charles A Murray's *The Bell Curve: Intelligence and Class Structure in American Life*
Eric Hoffer's *The True Believer: Thoughts on the Nature of Mass Movements*
Jane Jacobs's *The Death and Life of Great American Cities*
Robert Lucas's *Why Doesn't Capital Flow from Rich to Poor Countries?*
Jay Macleod's *Ain't No Makin' It: Aspirations and Attainment in a Low Income Neighborhood*
Elaine May's *Homeward Bound: American Families in the Cold War Era*
Douglas McGregor's *The Human Side of Enterprise*
C. Wright Mills's *The Sociological Imagination*

Thomas Piketty's *Capital in the Twenty-First Century*
Robert D. Putman's *Bowling Alone*
David Riesman's *The Lonely Crowd: A Study of the Changing American Character*
Edward Said's *Orientalism*
Joan Wallach Scott's *Gender and the Politics of History*
Theda Skocpol's *States and Social Revolutions*
Max Weber's *The Protestant Ethic and the Spirit of Capitalism*

THEOLOGY

Augustine's *Confessions*
Benedict's *Rule of St Benedict*
Gustavo Gutiérrez's *A Theology of Liberation*
Carole Hillenbrand's *The Crusades: Islamic Perspectives*
David Hume's *Dialogues Concerning Natural Religion*
Immanuel Kant's *Religion within the Boundaries of Mere Reason*
Ernst Kantorowicz's *The King's Two Bodies: A Study in Medieval Political Theology*
Søren Kierkegaard's *The Sickness Unto Death*
C. S. Lewis's *The Abolition of Man*
Saba Mahmood's *The Politics of Piety: The Islamic Revival and the Feminist Subject*
Baruch Spinoza's *Ethics*
Keith Thomas's *Religion and the Decline of Magic*

COMING SOON

Chris Argyris's *The Individual and the Organisation*
Seyla Benhabib's *The Rights of Others*
Walter Benjamin's *The Work Of Art in the Age of Mechanical Reproduction*
John Berger's *Ways of Seeing*
Pierre Bourdieu's *Outline of a Theory of Practice*
Mary Douglas's *Purity and Danger*
Roland Dworkin's *Taking Rights Seriously*
James G. March's *Exploration and Exploitation in Organisational Learning*
Ikujiro Nonaka's *A Dynamic Theory of Organizational Knowledge Creation*
Griselda Pollock's *Vision and Difference*
Amartya Sen's *Inequality Re-Examined*
Susan Sontag's *On Photography*
Yasser Tabbaa's *The Transformation of Islamic Art*
Ludwig von Mises's *Theory of Money and Credit*

Printed in the United States
by Baker & Taylor Publisher Services